Population Vulnerability and Evacuation Challenges in California for the SAFRR Tsunami Scenario

Open-File Report 2013–1170–I
California Geological Survey Special Report 229

U.S. Department of the Interior
U.S. Geological Survey

COVER—Photograph of Huntington Beach, California, from the City of Huntington Beach (2012), which states that all of its website content is public information.

The SAFRR (Science Application for Risk Reduction) Tsunami Scenario

Stephanie Ross and Lucile Jones, Editors

Population Vulnerability and Evacuation Challenges in California for the SAFRR Tsunami Scenario

By Nathan Wood, Jamie Ratliff, Jeff Peters, and Kimberley Shoaf

Open-File Report 2013–1170-I

California Geological Survey Special Report 229

U.S. Department of the Interior
U.S. Geological Survey

U.S. Department of the Interior
SALLY JEWELL, Secretary

U.S. Geological Survey
Suzette M. Kimball, Acting Director

U.S. Geological Survey, Reston, Virginia 2013

For product and ordering information:
World Wide Web: http://www.usgs.gov/pubprod
Telephone: 1-888-ASK-USGS

For more information on the USGS—the Federal source for science about the Earth,
its natural and living resources, natural hazards, and the environment:
World Wide Web: http://www.usgs.gov
Telephone: 1-888-ASK-USGS

Suggested citation:
Wood, N., Ratliff, J., Peters, J., and Shoaf, K., 2013, Population vulnerability and evacuation challenges in California for the SAFRR tsunami scenario, chap. I in Ross, S.L., and Jones, L.M., eds., The SAFRR (Science Application for Risk Reduction) Tsunami Scenario: U.S. Geological Survey Open-File Report 2013–1170, 53 p., http://pubs.usgs.gov/of/2013/1170/i/.

STATE OF CALIFORNIA
EDMUND G. BROWN JR.
GOVERNOR

THE NATURAL RESOURCES AGENCY
JOHN LAIRD
SECRETARY FOR RESOURCES

DEPARTMENT OF CONSERVATION
MARK NECHODOM
DIRECTOR

CALIFORNIA GEOLOGICAL SURVEY
JOHN G. PARRISH, Ph.D.
STATE GEOLOGIST

Contents

Figures

Tables

Population Vulnerability and Evacuation Challenges in California for the SAFRR Tsunami Scenario

By Nathan Wood[1], Jamie Ratliff[1], Jeff Peters[1], and Kimberley Shoaf[2]

Abstract

The SAFRR tsunami scenario models the impacts of a hypothetical yet plausible tsunami associated with a magnitude 9.1 megathrust earthquake east of the Alaska Peninsula. This report summarizes community variations in population vulnerability and potential evacuation challenges to the tsunami. The most significant public-health concern for California coastal communities during a distant-source tsunami is the ability to evacuate people out of potential inundation zones. Fatalities from the SAFRR tsunami scenario could be low if emergency managers can implement an effective evacuation in the time between tsunami generation and arrival, as well as keep people from entering tsunami-prone areas until all-clear messages can be delivered. This will be challenging given the estimated 91,956 residents, 81,277 employees, as well as numerous public venues, dependent-population facilities, community-support businesses, and high-volume beaches that are in the 79 incorporated communities and 17 counties that have land in the scenario tsunami-inundation zone.

Although all coastal communities face some level of threat from this scenario, the highest concentrations of people in the scenario tsunami-inundation zone are in Long Beach, San Diego, Newport Beach, Huntington Beach, and San Francisco. Communities also vary in the prevalent categories of populations that are in scenario tsunami-inundation zones, such as residents in Long Beach, employees in San Francisco, tourists at public venues in Santa Cruz, and beach or park visitors in unincorporated Los Angeles County. Certain communities have higher percentages of groups that may need targeted outreach and preparedness training, such as renters, the very young and very old, and individuals with limited English-language skills or no English-language skills at all. Sustained education and targeted evacuation messaging is also important at several high-occupancy public venues in the scenario tsunami-inundation zone (for example, city and county beaches, State or national parks, and amusement parks). Evacuations will be challenging, particularly for certain dependent-care populations, such as patients at hospitals and children at schools and daycare centers. We estimate that approximately 8,678 of the 91,956 residents in the scenario inundation zone are likely to need publicly provided shelters in the short term. Information presented in this report could be used to support emergency managers in their efforts to identify where additional preparedness and outreach activities may be needed to manage risks associated with California tsunamis.

---

[1] U.S. Geological Survey
[2] Center for Public Health and Disasters, Fielding School of Public Health, University of California, Los Angeles

Introduction

The California coast is a prime location for residents, recreational opportunities, tourism-related businesses, and other commerce. In the event of a large tsunami, thousands of individuals will need to evacuate low-lying areas along the California coast and remain out of harm's way until public officials believe it is safe to return. For the SAFRR (Science Application for Risk Reduction) scenario tsunami associated with a magnitude 9.1 megathrust earthquake east of the Alaska Peninsula, California emergency managers and public-safety officials will have several hours between tsunami wave generation and arrival to initiate and coordinate evacuations. The hypothetical tsunami-producing earthquake is designed to occur at 11:57 AM PDT on Thursday 27 March 2014, which is 50 years after the 1964 M_w 9.2 Good Friday earthquake and tsunami that occurred in the Prince William Sound region of Alaska (U.S. Geological Survey, 2012). Tsunami wave travel times to California after the initial earthquake are estimated to range from 4 hours in northern California to almost 6 hours in southern California. This timing means that the tsunami warnings and wave arrivals would occur during a workday afternoon (Ross and others, 2013).

Although 4–6 hours may seem to be sufficient time to evacuate potential tsunami-inundation zones, there have been deaths in California from previous distant tsunamis (for example, 1946, 1960, 1964, and 2011). Evacuations will be challenging given the scale of the evacuation along the entire California coast, the size and dispersed nature of the populations in inundation zones, and the unique needs of the varied populations. Evacuation messages will need to be delivered repeatedly by multiple actors over multiple channels to a highly diverse audience with varying levels of tsunami-risk knowledge, such as residents, employees at a range of business types, patrons of local stores, tourists at public venues and beaches, and individuals at dependent-care facilities. Although consistent evacuation messages may be delivered, comprehension of the message and actions taken by at-risk individuals will vary because of language or cultural barriers, differences in risk tolerances, inconsistent understanding of what actions to take, and evacuation limitations due to personal mobility and timing (National Research Council, 2010).

The immediate concern of emergency managers will be the safety of the at-risk population over the duration of the tsunami waves. The first tsunami wave of this scenario may garner the most attention, but subsequent waves may be just as threatening, or more so depending on local conditions. The one death in California that resulted from the 2011 Tohoku earthquake and tsunami occurred after the first tsunami waves had come and gone (Barnard, 2011). In addition to concerns about survival and staying safe, the quality of life of individuals may be impacted by tsunamis. Closed beaches and shorefront businesses reduce recreational opportunities and revenue. Closed roads increase commuting times. Closed dependent-care facilities, such as schools and hospitals, directly impact children or patients and affect others who would need to become caregivers, such as the parents who cannot go back to work because their child's daycare center is closed.

To better understand the range of evacuation challenges that may arise from a tsunami associated with the SAFRR scenario earthquake east of the Alaska Peninsula, we assessed the geographic variations in exposure for populations in the scenario inundation zone. We focus on three questions:

· How many people may need to evacuate, and which communities have the highest numbers of people in the tsunami-inundation zone?
· Which individuals and population groups may have greater difficulty in preparing for and responding to a tsunami?
· How many people may need to use public shelters after the tsunami?

We focus on determining the number and types of various population groups in the SAFRR scenario tsunami-inundation zone, including residents, employees, visitors at public venues, dependent-care populations, business customers, and beach visitors. We also compare communities based on their at-risk populations and potential sheltering needs. Subsequent sections include an overview of potential public-health issues related to tsunamis, the geographic scope for our analysis, and results that address our three questions.

Public-Health Implications of a Distant-Source Tsunami

The potential loss of life from this scenario tsunami is low in California given the estimated amount of time before waves arrive, but it is possible if individuals choose not to evacuate hazardous areas, do not understand tsunami warnings, are unable to evacuate for various reasons, or are indirectly impacted owing to the loss of healthcare services. Direct impacts to individuals include injuries and illnesses that result from contact with tsunami waves, such as drowning and/or trauma from being struck by debris in the tsunami flow. Indirect impacts include secondary infections resulting from injuries or from living conditions following the disasters, such as an increase in pneumonia from water aspiration, as well as cellulitis from exposure of breaks in the skin to contaminated water (Doocy and others, 2009; Nagamatsu and others, 2011). Other indirect impacts to individuals include emotional and psychological effects, such as anxiety, depression, or other psychological pathologies (Shoaf and Rottman, 2000). In addition, any disruption to the healthcare system will impact an individual's health by introducing complications to preexisting conditions (Shoaf and Rottman, 2000; Nagamatsu and others, 2011). Healthcare-service disruptions can result from direct damage to facilities, flooding that shuts down certain floors of facilities, or loss of the surrounding lifelines, such as power and water.

Coastal communities will have approximately 4 hours in northern California and almost 6 hours in southern California after initial ground shaking begins in Alaska to evaluate the situation and evacuate tsunami-prone areas for the SAFRR tsunami scenario. Based on past distant tsunamis that have struck California, this may be sufficient time to evacuate most people in low-lying areas. The SAFRR distant-source tsunami scenario involves larger waves than those that have been recorded for historical tsunamis. Future evacuation success will be determined by the efficiency of the warning-message communication network, the effectiveness of emergency decisionmaking at the local level, and the ability of local public-safety officials to effectively engage the public to evacuate. However, even with well-executed evacuations, loss of life is possible and has happened during distant tsunamis in the following situations:

· Individuals in remote areas fail to evacuate because they do not receive warning messages, such as the drowning of a family camping on an Oregon beach during the 1964 Good Friday tsunami.
· Individuals return prematurely to hazardous areas because they do not realize there are multiple waves, such as the drowning in California near the Klamath River during the 2011 Tohoku tsunami and several deaths in Crescent City, Calif., during the 1964 Good Friday tsunami.
· Individuals are struck by falling equipment while trying to secure boats or other assets, which happened to one man in Morro Bay, Calif., during the 1960 Chilean tsunami and to another man in the Port of Los Angeles, Calif., during the 1964 Good Friday tsunami.
· Individuals have limited mobility, such as the drowning of an elderly man in Santa Cruz, Calif., who was unable to move quickly to high ground during the 1946 Aleutian tsunami.

·   Individuals with preexisting health complications become overly stressed, such as one woman who died of a heart attack in Seaside, Ore., after waves associated with the 1964 Good Friday tsunami struck her home (all examples from Lander and others, 1993).

Additional evacuation challenges will exist for those considered to be "at-risk populations," which are defined as individuals who may have additional functional needs related to communication, medical care, maintaining independence, supervision, or transportation. These functional needs may make it more difficult to evacuate the inundation zone in a timely manner. At-risk populations include children, senior citizens, and pregnant women, as well as individuals who have disabilities, live in institutional settings, are from diverse cultures, have limited English proficiency, lack transportation options, have chronic medical disorders, or have pharmacological dependencies. These populations will warrant additional evacuation time and unique response and relief procedures (U.S. Department of Health and Human Services, 2012).

Geographic Scope of Analysis

This analysis focuses on comparing population vulnerability to the scenario tsunami among the 77 incorporated cities, 2 incorporated towns, and 17 California counties that intersect the scenario tsunami-inundation zone (fig. 1) as discussed by the SAFRR Tsunami Modeling Working Group in this report. Incorporated cities and counties are delineated by 2010 census place boundaries (U.S. Census Bureau, 2010). The coastal counties also contain 52 unincorporated communities, as delineated by census-designated place boundaries, which intersect the scenario tsunami-inundation zone. Because emergency services in these areas are provided by county offices, results for these places and for other county land not in incorporated cities are aggregated and reported as "remaining land" for a given county.

The scenario tsunami-inundation mapping was limited to the significant population and economic centers along the California coast and does not represent potential inundation along the entire coastline, as was also the case with the statewide maximum tsunami-inundation zone summarized by Wilson and others (2008) and Barberopoulou and others (2009). Percentages related to remaining county lands in the scenario tsunami-inundation zone might have been larger if the whole coast was mapped; however, we believe this difference is not substantial based on a visual inspection of the scenario-inundation zone and satellite imagery of the California coast. Unmapped areas are primarily places with low populations owing to their ruggedness or remoteness. Differences in estimated amounts and percentages in each jurisdiction and the remaining unincorporated county land for the area mapped in the SAFRR tsunami scenario versus the entire California coastline are likely less than 1 percent.

Figure 1. *A*, Map of coastline, counties, and incorporated communities with land in the SAFRR scenario tsunami-inundation zone. *B*, Enlargement of the San Francisco Bay area. *C*, Enlargement of Los Angeles and Orange counties. Geospatial boundaries for maps acquired from Cal-Atlas Geospatial Clearinghouse (2013). Scenario tsunami-inundation zone courtesy of the California Geological Survey.

This analysis is based on the presence of populations and businesses in the scenario tsunami-inundation zone using various datasets and is tallied using geographic information system (GIS) tools. Results are not engineering-based loss estimates for any particular facility. Instead, the analysis focused on determining if geospatial points (for example, businesses) or polygons (for example, census blocks) are inside the inundation zone. If population polygons overlapped hazard polygons, final population values were adjusted proportionately by using the spatial ratio of each sliver within the tsunami-inundation zone. Third-quartile values are identified throughout this report to more easily identify communities that are in the top 25 percent of any one category. Inventories cannot be considered mortality estimates because aspects of individual perceptions and preparedness levels before a tsunami, and the adaptive capacity of individuals during a response, are excluded from this analysis (Turner and others, 2003). Potential mortality would only match reported inventories if all at-risk individuals were unaware of tsunami risks and what to do after being warned of an imminent threat, and if they failed to take protective measures to evacuate. This assumption is unrealistic, given the current level of tsunami-awareness efforts in California (California Emergency Management Agency, 2012) and recent distant-tsunami experiences in 2010 and 2011. Exposure counts for the various population groups also should not be combined because of the likelihood of overlap; for example, the young resident who attends daycare also may be a customer at a local store and a visitor of a local beach. This analysis is intended to help emergency managers understand where evacuations may be most challenging along the California coast and where evacuation messages and approaches may need to be tailored to address local needs.

Magnitude and Hotspots of Population Exposure

Residents

The scenario tsunami-inundation zone is home to an estimated 91,956 residents in 40,120 households, each total representing less than 1 percent of the residents and households in the 17 counties. This estimate is based on an overlay of geospatial data representing the scenario tsunami-inundation zone, community boundaries, and block-level population counts compiled for the 2010 census (U.S. Census Bureau, 2012). The number of residents in the tsunami-inundation zone varies greatly across the 17 counties (fig. 2). The cities of Long Beach and San Diego have the greatest number of residents in the tsunami-inundation zone (12,933 and 12,751 residents, respectively). There are 14 communities and unincorporated land in four counties that each have more than 1,000 residents in the scenario tsunami-inundation zone. For most communities, the scenario inundation area directly affects less than 10 percent of the residential population; however larger percentages exist in the cities of Belvedere, Del Mar, and Coronado (40, 15, and 11 percent, respectively). Eleven percent of the at-risk residents live in unincorporated areas, indicating a need for education and preparedness planning in less developed areas.

One residential group of particular concern in this scenario estimate is made up of residents living on boats in the various marinas. It is highly likely that these vessels would be damaged, representing life-safety issues during the tsunami and sheltering needs after the event. Many vessels used as residences may not be seaworthy. Live-aboard residents who can go offshore to protect themselves and their boats during a tsunami may have insufficient food, water, and fuel to use while they wait for all-clear messages to return to shore; therefore, relief efforts will be needed to care for these individuals.

Employees

Employees present an evacuation challenge because they may be unaware of tsunami hazards or proper evacuation strategies, especially if they do not live in tsunami-inundation zones. They also may rely on business owners for information if they lack social connections to the community. The scenario tsunami-inundation zone contains an estimated 81,277 employees at 7,343 businesses in the 17 counties. This is based on an overlay of the tsunami-inundation zone and the 2011 Infogroup Employer Database (Infogroup, 2011). Our counts serve as approximations because we were unable to field-verify locations for each of the 1,001,413 businesses from the Infogroup Employer Database used in our 17-county study area. Visual interpretation of imagery, including Google Maps and 1-meter 2010 National Agriculture Imagery Program imagery (Cal-Atlas Geospatial Clearinghouse, 2013), was used to verify and correct business locations in the tsunami-inundation zone.

The greatest numbers of employees working within the scenario tsunami-inundation zone are in the cities of Long Beach (11,127), San Francisco (9,176), Newport Beach (7,967), and San Diego (6,726), reflecting the active ports and (or) waterfront tourism in each city (fig. 3). For most communities, the scenario inundation area directly affects less than 20 percent of the employee population. Exceptions include Belvedere (77 percent), Sausalito (56 percent), Tiburon (41 percent), and Crescent City (33 percent), where much larger percentages of the local workforce will need to evacuate.

The number of estimated employees in the scenario-inundation zone is likely to be low in the larger ports because of the dynamic nature and magnitude of employees that are associated with multiple port-related companies. For example, our economic data identifies each business location as a point (typically the primary mailbox), but employees at a port-related business could be distributed across a large area within a port complex. In addition, foreign or domestic ships may be docked in the ports during the tsunami, but onboard crew members are not accounted for in this analysis of employee exposure.

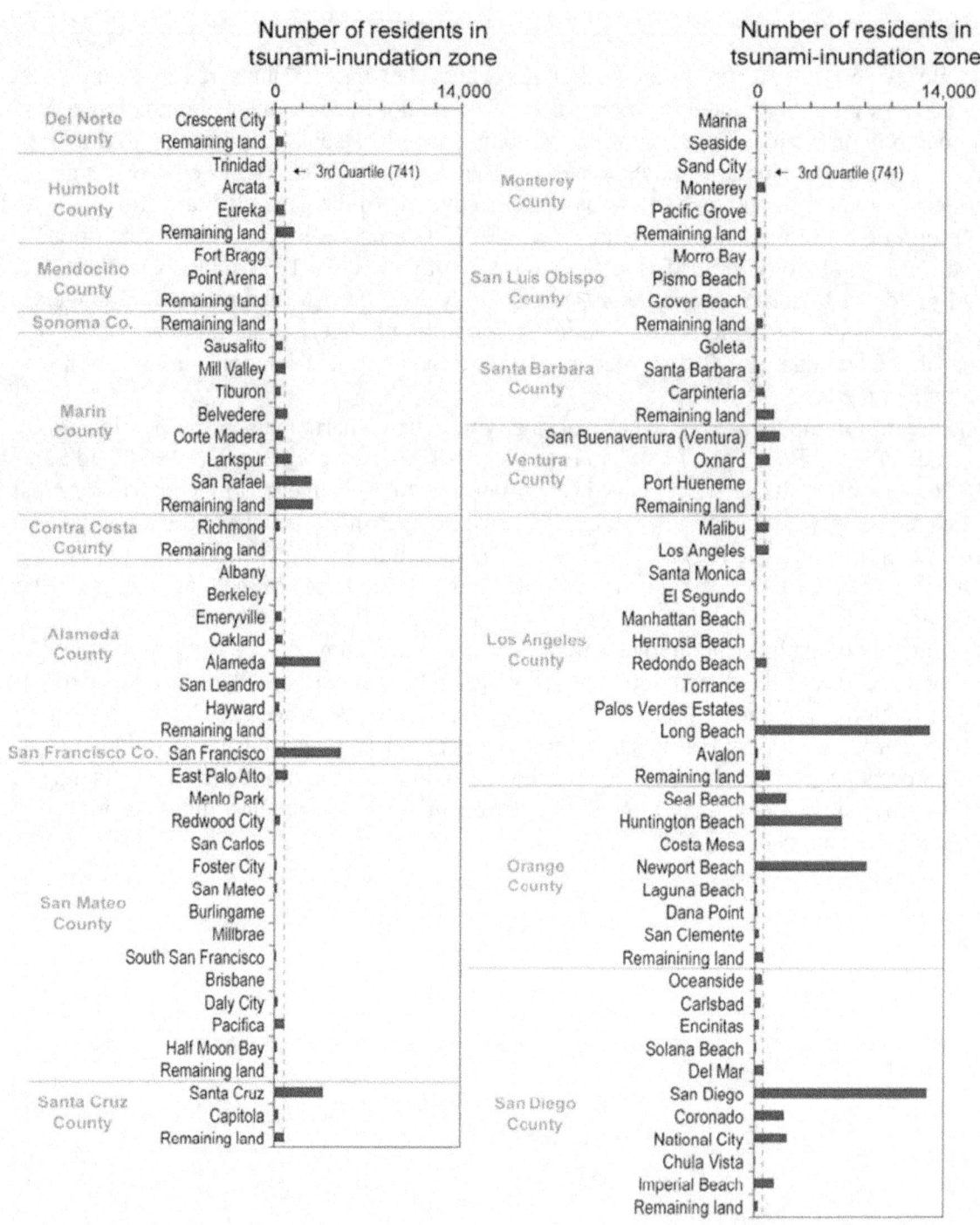

Figure 2. Plot showing number of residents in the SAFRR tsunami-inundation zone for the California coast. Co., county.

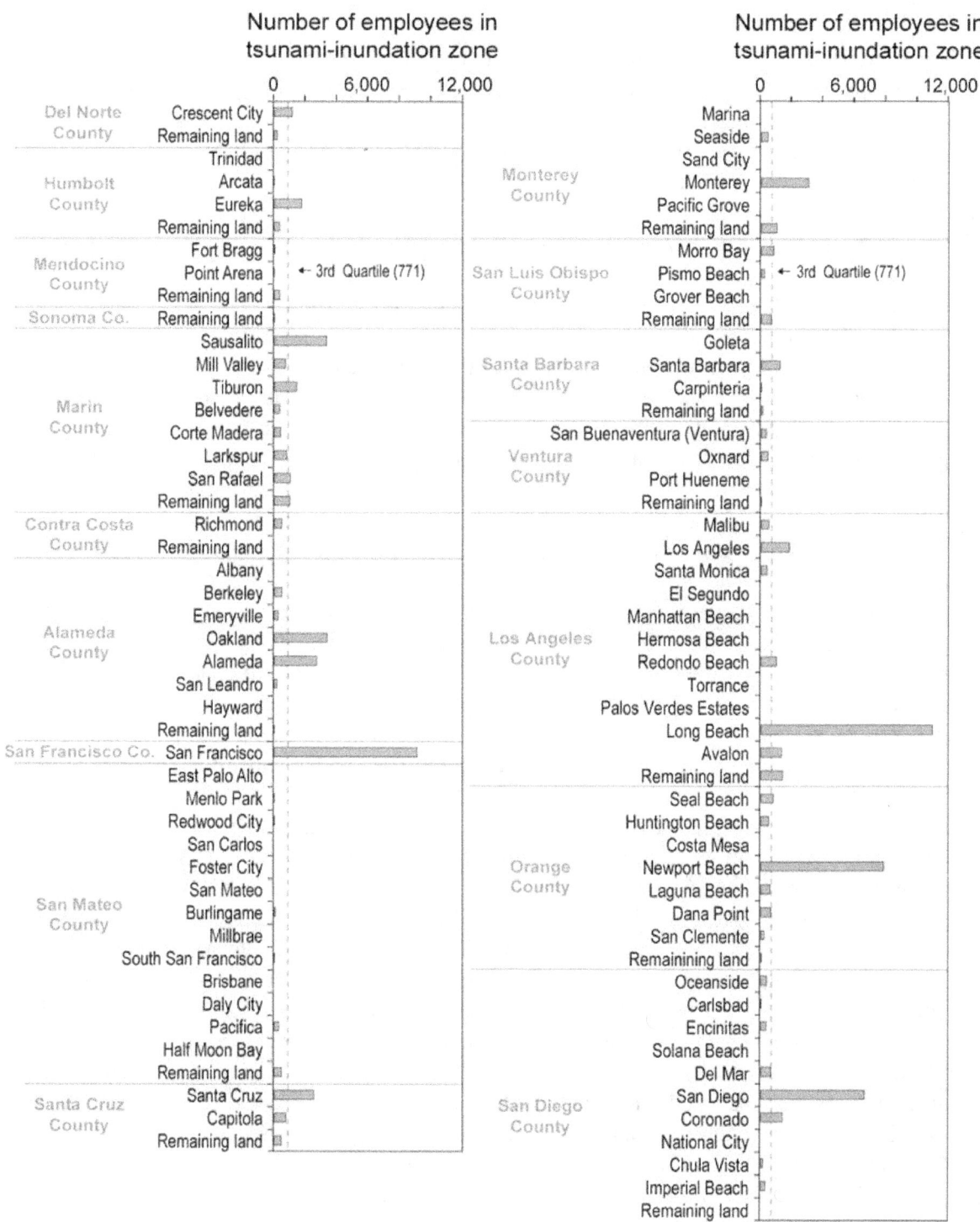

Figure 3. Plot showing number of employees in the SAFRR tsunami-inundation zone for the California coast. Co., county.

Business Customers

The primary business sectors in the scenario tsunami-inundation zone along the California coast are accommodation and food services (32 percent) and retail trade (12 percent), suggesting that a high number of customers also will need to evacuate (fig. 4). This analysis is based on the number of employees associated with North American Industry Classification System (NAICS) codes for businesses in the 2011 Infogroup Employer Database (see appendix A of Wood, 2007, for a listing of the codes; Infogroup, 2011). The number of employees associated with each business is considered a better indicator of business sectors and market trends than the number of businesses (Bureau of Labor Statistics, 2010).

To identify community hotspots for business customers or visitors, we subjectively grouped the multiple NAICS classes based on customer potential. We considered businesses with high onsite customer potential to include NAICS classes for accommodation and food services; arts, entertainment and recreation; educational services; healthcare and social assistance; and retail trade. We consider businesses with low onsite customer potential to include NAICS classes for administrative support and waste management; agriculture, forestry, fishing, and hunting; construction; finance and insurance; information; management of companies; manufacturing; mining; professional, scientific, and technical services; public administration; real-estate rental and leasing; transportation and warehousing utilities; wholesale trade and other, nonclassified businesses.

The majority of employees (67 percent) across the entire study area work for businesses that we think have a high customer potential (represented by the dotted line in figure 5). The stacked bar graphs in figure 5 reflect only the relative percentage of employees among the two business groups and not the absolute number of employees in the various groups. The lack of a stacked bar graph for a community (for example, Trinidad, Albany, and Torrance) indicates that there are no employees, according to our regional economic data, in the scenario tsunami-inundation zone of these communities.

Several communities, such as San Francisco and Corte Madera, have percentages similar to the statewide trend (fig. 5). In other communities, onsite customer potential at businesses in the tsunami-inundation zone is higher. For example, we estimate that all businesses in the tsunami-inundation zones of Point Arena, Burlingame, Seaside, Santa Monica, Laguna Beach, and Carlsbad have a high customer potential. In communities where at-risk businesses have a high customer potential, tsunami evacuations may be more difficult because evacuees may be unaware of the tsunami threat and unaware of what to do in the event of a tsunami. Successful tsunami-outreach efforts before an event and evacuations during an event will require emergency managers to collaborate with the private sector to reach visitor and tourist populations. This is especially important if emergency managers are to reach tourists, who traditionally are difficult to engage in long-term education, at beaches near waterfront businesses.

Although not as frequent, there are communities where the majority of the employees in the tsunami-inundation zone are at businesses have low onsite customer potential, including Fort Bragg, Menlo Park, and the unincorporated areas of Humboldt and Alameda Counties (fig. 5). In these types of communities, pre-event outreach and evacuation messaging to employees could leverage local knowledge and could be delivered through business meetings, neighborhood associations, and community fairs. If at-risk businesses are industrial, further discussions could help determine if employee evacuations would be hindered by the presence of hazardous materials, heavy machinery, seasonal equipment (for example, crab pots in a harbor), or other materials (for example, timber).

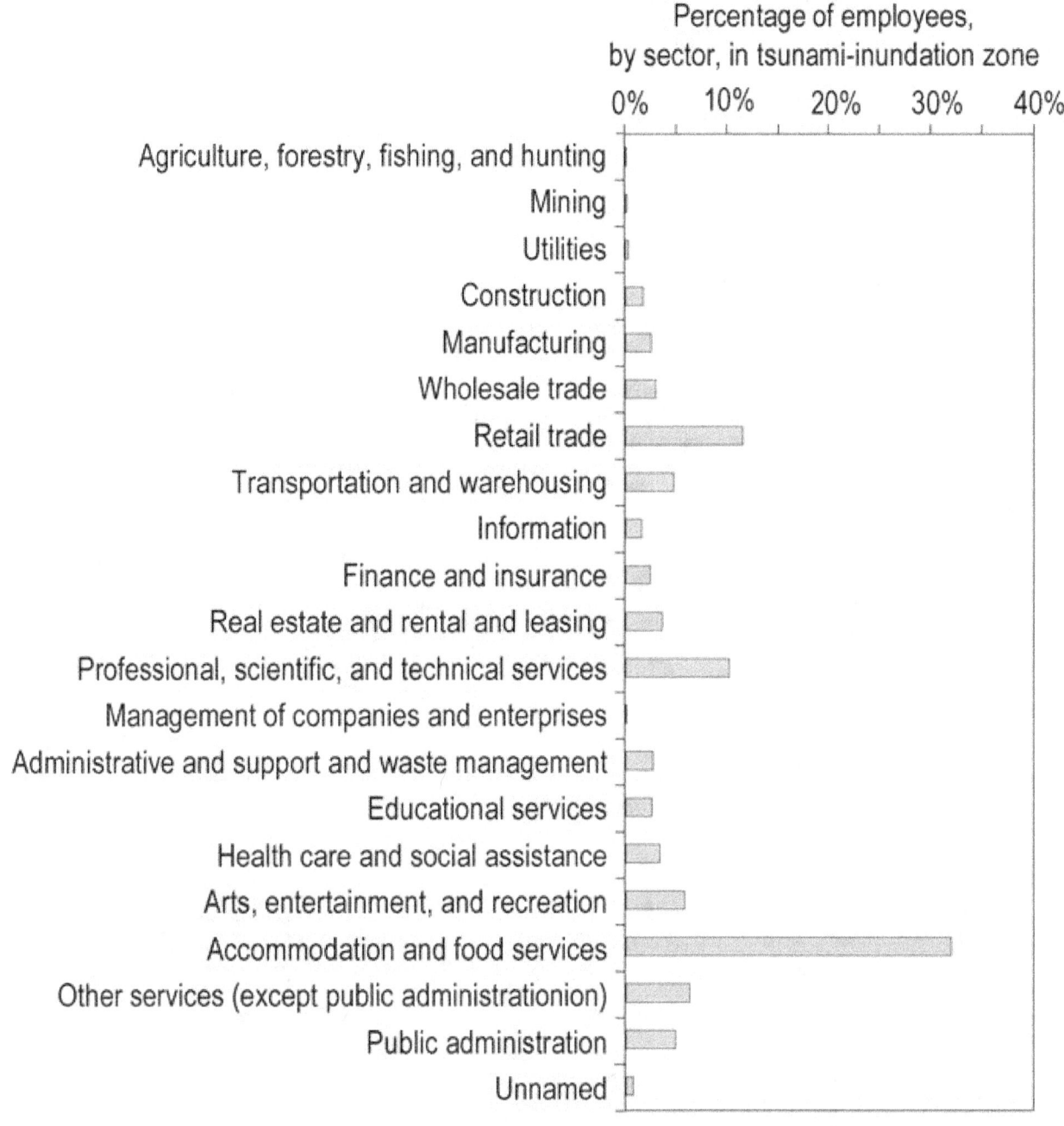

Figure 4. Plot showing percentage of employees, by business sector, in the SAFRR tsunami-inundation zone, California coast.

Figure 5. Plot showing percentage of employees at businesses in the SAFRR tsunami-inundation zone, California coast, with low and high customer or visitor potential. Co., county.

Community-Support Businesses

To provide further insight into the number of people in the scenario inundation zone, we used NAICS codes in the 2011 Infogroup Employer Database to identify certain types of businesses with customers or visitors, specifically community-support businesses, dependent-care facilities, and public venues. The high number of businesses and the dynamic nature of populations at these locations preclude our ability to determine exact visitor counts at each business; therefore, discussions of these locations are limited to the number of venues and facilities. The first category—community support—includes businesses that attract significant populations throughout a workday because they provide basic necessities, primarily to residents (although visitors may use them also). These community-support businesses include

· Banks or credit unions;
· Civil or social organizations, including social clubs, after-school programs, and lodges;
· Retail, including grocery stores, wholesale warehouse stores, and home-improvement stores;
· Government offices, including Federal, State, and local government offices, police and fire departments, courts and legal offices, and international-affairs offices;
· Libraries, including city, Federal, institutional, public, and State libraries;
· Mailing and shipping services, including U.S. Post Offices and commercial shipping facilities; and
· Religious organizations, including churches, church organizations, mosques, mediation organizations, clergy, convents and monasteries, retreat houses, spiritualists, synagogues, and places of worship (nontheistic).

There are many businesses that primarily provide community support in the tsunami-inundation zone, including 81 civil or social organizations, 34 religious organizations, 11 libraries, 139 government offices, 29 banks and credit unions, and 2,706 retail businesses (fig. 6). The greatest numbers of community-support businesses in the tsunami-inundation zone are in the cities of Newport Beach, Long Beach, San Diego, San Francisco, Sausalito, and Monterey. The majority of community-support businesses in the tsunami-inundation zone are retail businesses.

As discussed earlier in this report, tsunami warnings for this scenario will likely come during the workday, with first waves arriving approximately 4 hours later. Because many people are at community-support businesses or organizations during the workday, they will likely receive warning information while at these locations. This may complicate evacuations because customers may be aware of tsunami threats only from the perspective of their homes and, therefore, are not fully aware of evacuation procedures, or even tsunami potential, when they are out running errands or attending a religious service. Pre-event education of business owners on how to coordinate evacuations out of their stores to high ground will be important for minimizing any potential confusion during an evacuation.

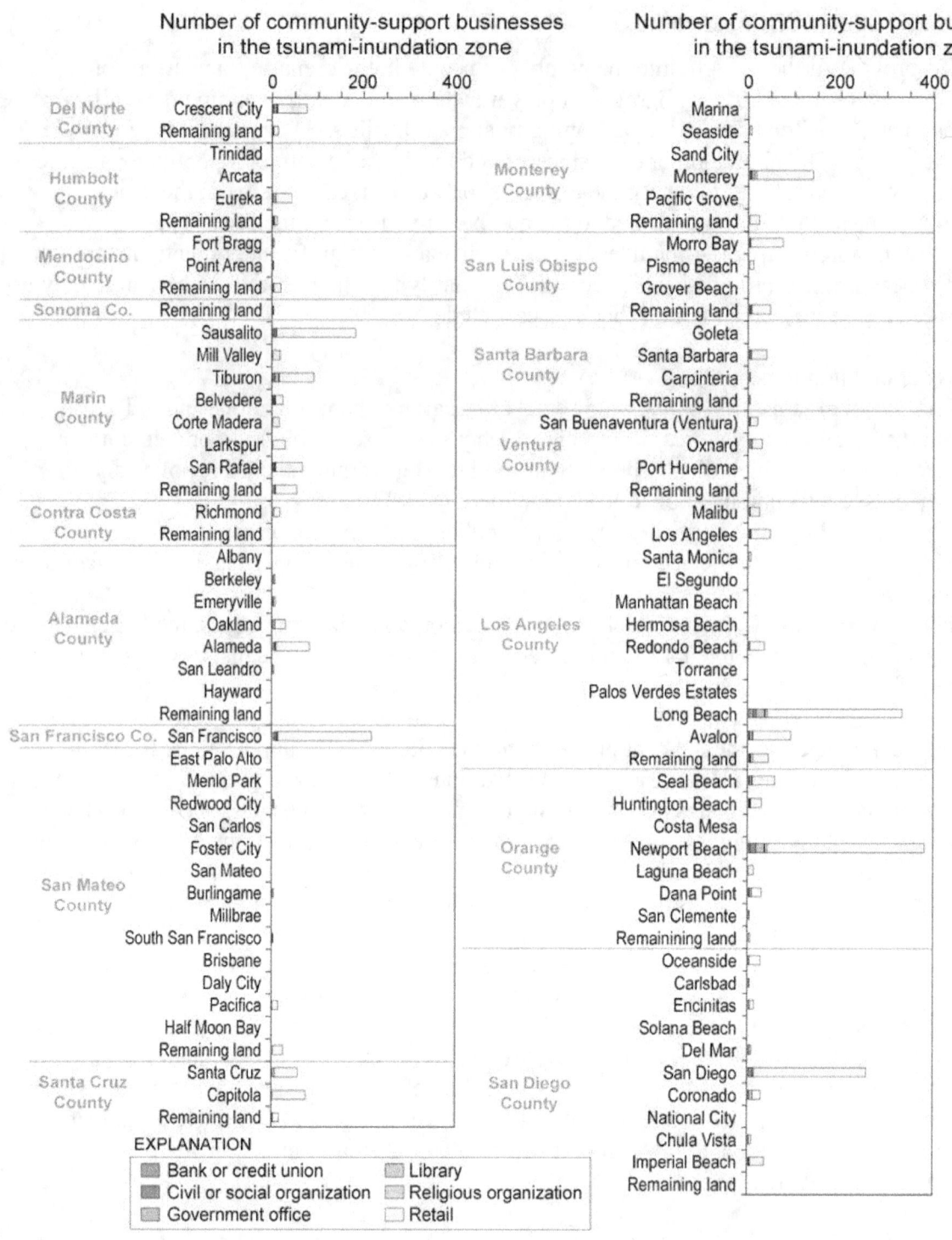

Figure 6. Plot showing number of community-support businesses and organizations in the SAFRR tsunami-inundation zone, California Coast. Co., county.

Dependent-Care Facilities

Dependent-care facilities contain individuals who would require assistance to evacuate and include

· Medical centers, including hospitals, psychiatric and substance-abuse hospitals, mental-health services and psychiatric treatment facilities, and clinics;
· Eldercare services, including adult-care facilities, hospices, nursing homes, rest homes, retirement communities, adult homes, senior citizens' services, residential care homes, and adult daycare centers;
· Child services, including group homes, foster care, childcare centers, preschools and nursery schools (both public and private), and after-school recreational facilities;
· Schools, including religious schools, public and private schools, schools with special academics, and home-schooling centers;
· Correctional institutions, including State and Federal facilities; and
· Medical and health services, including offices for general practitioners, pediatricians, obstetricians and gynecologists, chiropractors, and acupuncturists.

A substantial number of dependent-population facilities are in the tsunami-inundation zone, including 29 schools and education-related facilities, 30 child-service facilities, 7 eldercare facilities, 415 offices of physicians or other medical personnel, and 17 medical centers (fig. 7). Most of the dependent-population facilities in the tsunami-inundation zone are in the city of Long Beach, the majority of which are medical- and health-service providers. Other communities with numerous dependent-care facilities in the tsunami-inundation zone include Mill Valley, Sausalito, and Newport Beach (with the primary type of facility providing medical and health services in each community). The majority of schools or school-related educational facilities in the tsunami-inundation zone are in Marin County (14 of the 29 education facilities in the inundation zone). The majority of medical centers in the tsunami-inundation zone are in Marin and Orange Counties (6 and 5 facilities, respectively).

Additional evacuation planning may be required in communities with large numbers of dependent-population facilities because of the limited mobility of certain groups at these facilities, such as those in schools and nursing homes. Parents may attempt to enter tsunami-prone areas to retrieve children from schools and daycare centers or adult children may attempt to enter tsunami-prone areas to retrieve their parents from eldercare facilities, and both situations present additional evacuation issues for facility managers. In addition to unique evacuation and relief issues, many dependent-population facilities represent critical social services that, if lost, could slow community recovery following an extreme event. For example, the loss of daycare centers could keep parents at home, thereby slowing business recovery.

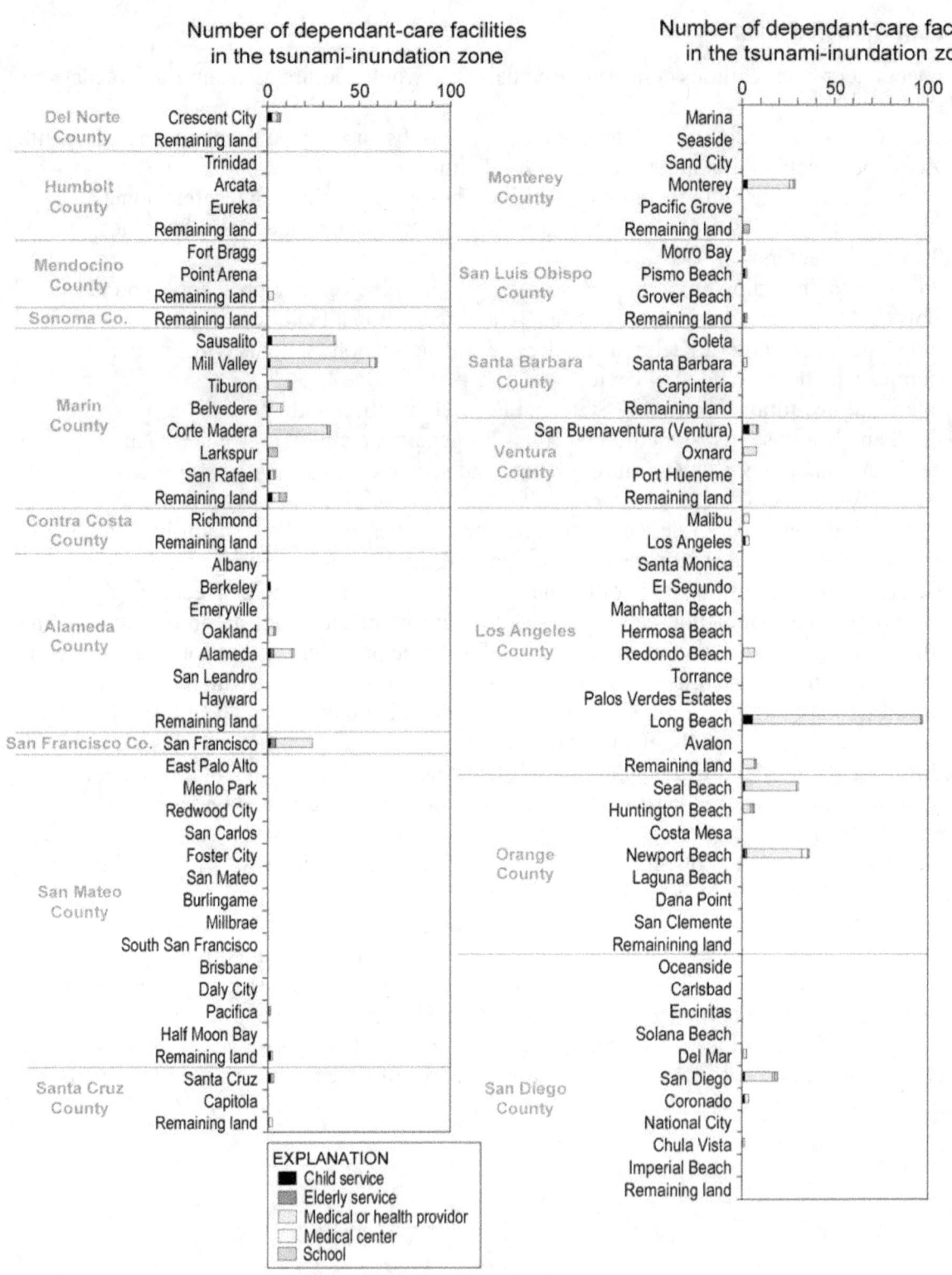

Figure 7. Plot showing number of dependent-care facilities in the SAFRR tsunami-inundation zone, California coast. Co., county.

Evacuation Challenges of Healthcare Facilities

Hospitals in the tsunami-inundation zone may have difficulty evacuating some patients in the 4 – 6 hour window before wave arrival. Emergency evacuations out of unsafe buildings to nearby open areas have been completed in 30–90 minutes, but this has been in situations where imminent danger to patients is greater than that faced by moving them (for example, fires). However, a well-coordinated evacuation that removes patients from unsafe conditions to a new hospital can take 6 – 8 hours or more.

Several recent evacuations illustrate the difference between simply evacuating the building and getting patients appropriate care elsewhere. Following the Northridge earthquake, one hospital felt that their patient population was in immediate danger from the building damage, and they evacuated 334 patients, including intensive-care patients, out of the building to an open area outside of the hospital in 2 hours (Schultz and others, 2003). Comprehensive evacuations that included moving patients to new facilities took between 9 and 19 hours to complete for the 6 hospitals that completely evacuated their facilities following the same earthquake (Schultz and others, 2003). Similar evacuations took place during Tropical Storm Allison in 2001, when the Texas Medical Center evacuated a great number of patients quickly out of the building, but then took more than 12 hours to transport them to definitive-care facilities (Parson, 2002). With a great deal of planning and coordination, the University of California, Los Angeles, Medical Center transferred 350 patients from an old building to a new facility across the street in 8 hours. This was accomplished by not admitting any new elective patients either the day before or the day of the transfer and by having a full staff at both facilities to maintain levels of care, ensure full functionality at both facilities, and provide additional transport staff (Groves, 2008). During Hurricane Charley in 2004, evacuating 120 patients from a Florida hospital to another facility took more than 6 hours and took more than a day at another facility to move 10 patients (Kuba and others, 2004).

The time needed to complete an evacuation is highly dependent on the level of coordination, the availability of appropriate transportation, and the availability of qualified personnel for transferring patients. Coordination during evacuations is critical to ensure that no single facility is overloaded with transfer patients, as well as for centralized tracking of patients so that family members can find them following the event. Transportation options may include buses or vans for those who are ambulatory, wheelchair-adaptable vans for some patients, and ambulances with basic or advanced life-support capacities for critical or intensive-care patients. Without the proper level of onboard medical support, a patient's health is jeopardized. For example, 4 ventilator-dependent patients died during hospital evacuations during Tropical Storm Allison, and 2 additional patients died within 24 hours (Rother, 2001). In addition, some patients may not be able to be moved immediately, such as patients undergoing dialysis (typically a 3–5 hour procedure) or undergoing surgery, either in a hospital or outpatient surgical center.

Staffing during evacuations is a significant challenge because many patients cannot simply walk out of a building to safe areas. This is an issue at hospitals where staff-to-patient ratios are not equal. It is also an issue at assisted-living facilities and senior citizen complexes where residents have fewer health needs than those in hospitals, but facilities have fewer full-time staff onsite at any one time. Nursing-facility residents are also at risk of not being able to evacuate in a timely manner because, although skilled nursing facilities are required to have an evacuation plan by regulation, many nursing facilities have not exercised those plans (Kuba and others, 2004). It is highly probable that most California nursing facilities have not contemplated a tsunami evacuation, and that the most likely scenario envisioned is a fire.

Potential Impacts Due to Loss of Healthcare Services

The impact of the tsunami on the healthcare and community infrastructure also can have a significant effect on the health of the population. Healthcare services that are in the tsunami-inundation zone will not be available to provide health services to the population for a significant period of time following the event. Following Tropical Storm Allison, the University of Texas Medical Center had power restored in less than 3 weeks, but the facility was not fully functional for more than 6 weeks (Parson, 2002). The potential loss of hospitals, doctors' offices, clinics, and dialysis centers can have a significant impact on the accessibility of healthcare services for the entire region. Although the tsunami-inundation zone is a small percentage of the region, the California healthcare system functions at full capacity practically every day; therefore, any reduction of capacity can have an impact on the entire system.

Health services also are a personal matter, and many people may forgo care until their preferred provider is available. For at-risk populations, any delay in seeking medical care may have a detrimental effect on their health status. Following the 2011 Tohoku tsunami, it was estimated that at least 282 people died from deteriorating chronic disease conditions due to a lack of access to medical care. The Japan Ministry of Health, Labor and Welfare reported that 500 deaths could have been prevented if regular healthcare services, as delivered under normal circumstances, had been promptly provided (Nagamatsu and others, 2011).

Loss of infrastructure, such as transportation routes, electricity, and water, can impact the health of the population. Although power may not be disrupted in a significant way, loss of power in parts of the community can still impact the health of the population. Any power loss in excess of 4 hours can have an impact on the health of certain parts of the population. Four hours is the timeframe in which food that is not kept at temperature begins to present a health risk (U.S. Department of Agriculture, 2012). Individuals who rely on medical equipment (for example, ventilators, powered wheelchairs, and oxygen condensers) are also at significant risk when the power fails. Many energy-dependent pieces of equipment have an internal battery to keep them functioning for some period of time, but this time period runs from about 45 minutes to a few hours. External batteries provide additional time, but generally less than 8 hours. Without back-up power, failure of this equipment is a life-threatening event (Kailes, 2009).

Homeless Population

The homeless population is another dependent population that would be at risk from future tsunamis and would likely need assistance to evacuate. There is limited data on homeless populations for the entire California coast, therefore, a complete inventory is not possible for this tsunami scenario. To provide some insight on emergency-management issues related to homeless people, we highlight data from a 2011 homeless-count report produced by the Los Angeles Homeless Services Authority for the greater Los Angeles area. The smallest unit of analysis in this report is a service planning area (SPA), and coastal areas in Los Angeles County that are at risk to future tsunamis are part of the West Los Angeles SPA and South Bay SPA (fig. 8), which were estimated to have approximately 6,788 and 3,512 homeless people, respectively. It is not known how many of these individuals would be in tsunami-inundation zones at the time of the scenario; however, it is likely there will be some homeless individuals on the beach or in nearby coastal parks when future tsunamis occur. Preexisting mental and physical conditions of some homeless individuals in the South Bay SPA and West Los Angeles SPA may present additional evacuation challenges to public safety officials, such as substance abuse (41 and 31 percent, respectively), mental illness (15 and 48 percent), physical disabilities (15 and 31 percent), or some combination of all of these attributes (Los Angeles Homeless Services Authority, 2011). In addition, once they are evacuated, homeless individuals may have nowhere to go and may require public shelters. Shelter volunteers may not be trained for meeting with the needs of the homeless population. Some homeless people may need to stay in the public shelters for longer periods of time than people who are part of other populations.

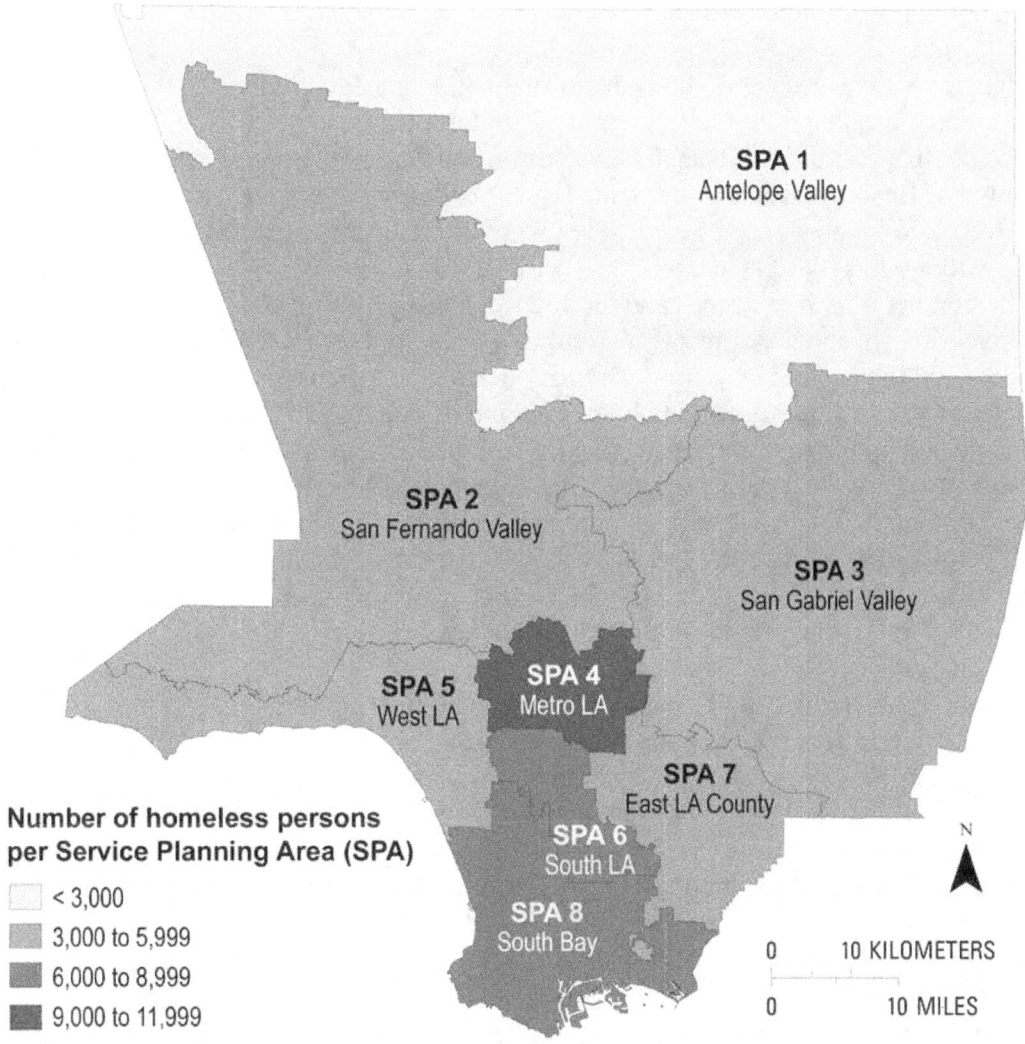

Figure 8. Map of estimated number of homeless people in Service Planning Areas (SPA) of Los Angeles county, California (based on Los Angeles Homeless Services Authority, 2011).

Public Venues

Tourists and other nonlocal populations are a significant element in coastal communities and often can outnumber residents and employees in tsunami-prone areas (Wood and Good, 2004). No consistent census count for visitors exists; therefore, the locations of public venues based on NAICS codes in the 2011 Infogroup Employer Database are used as an indicator of visitor populations. For this analysis, we consider public venues to include

- Entertainment centers, including aquariums, botanical gardens, casinos, theaters (including live and cinematic), and amusement parks;
- Colleges, including community colleges, private universities, and public universities;
- Marina and ferries, including recreational and fishing, vessel repair and storage, and yacht clubs; and
- Overnight accommodations, including hotels, inns, resorts, hostels, cabin rentals, bed and breakfasts, and student housing.

Many public venues are in the tsunami-inundation zone, including 167 overnight accommodations, 6 colleges, 79 marinas, and 311 entertainment centers (fig. 9). The highest numbers of public venues in the tsunami-inundation zone are in the cities of San Diego, Long Beach, Newport Beach, Sausalito, and Santa Cruz. As discussed earlier, visitors may not be fully aware of evacuation procedures, or even the potential for tsunamis, especially if they are coming from areas with no history of tsunamis.

The number of public venues and facilities in tsunami-prone areas of each community provides some insight about visitor populations, but does not capture the range in magnitudes. To better understand the number of visitors that may need to be evacuated during the scenario event, we estimated onsite visitor populations for certain public venues. To do this, we took visitor numbers provided by business owners (typically provided as annual or monthly counts) and adjusted them to represent a daily estimate for a Thursday in March using methods described by Dwight and others (2007). Their study of southern California beach attendance suggests that 5.2 percent of yearly visitors come in March and that 10 percent of visits occur on Thursdays. Because we are not aware of similar work for coastal businesses, we used these percentages to estimate attendance at the following public venues on a Thursday in March:

- Monterey Bay Aquarium, 2,437 people (Barret and others, 2012);
- Santa Cruz Beach Boardwalk, 3,900 people (Season Pass/Group Sales Office, oral commun., October 1, 2012);
- Santa Monica Pier, 9,095 people (Westman, 2011);
- The Long Beach Convention Center, 2,454 people (Convention Center Controller, oral commun., October 2, 2012); and
- Aquarium of the Pacific in Long Beach, 2,879 guests (Aquarium Vice President of Communications, oral commun., October 1, 2012).

Examples of other high-occupancy public venues in the scenario tsunami-inundation zone are

- Public piers with high-volume tourist populations in Santa Cruz, Redondo Beach, Santa Barbara, and Pismo Beach;
- The Catalina Casino in Avalon, which includes a 1,184-seat theater and a ballroom with a capacity of 1,400 people (Catalina Island Chamber of Commerce and Visitors Bureau, 2012);
- Waterfronts that serve as ports of call for cruises, such as the city of Avalon on Catalina Island, which receives tourists from five international cruise lines, including up to 2,000 passengers on a weekly basis from a single ship (Catalina Island Chamber of Commerce and Visitors Bureau, 2012);
- Del Mar Fairgrounds, which includes a racetrack and holds events year-round; and

- The Queen Mary ship in Long Beach, a popular tourist attraction that holds special events and has overnight accommodations.

Other high-occupancy public areas, such as SeaWorld theme park in San Diego and Cannery Row in Monterey, are near, but not in, the landward extent of the predicted scenario tsunami inundation zone. Whether or not evacuations would be called at these locations and others like them is a subject for further discussion between emergency managers and the business owners, given the uncertainty inherent in the tsunami modeling and the need to have sufficient time to evacuate before receiving full knowledge of the event.

Another category of public venues in the study area that attracts thousands of tourists are port terminals that serve cruise ships, including the World Cruise Center at the Port of Los Angeles that serves 12 different cruise lines (Pacific Cruise Ship Terminals, 2012) and the Long Beach Cruise Terminal that primarily serves Carnival cruises. Together, these cruise terminals see more than 300 cruise departures every year (Cruisetimetables, 2012). Thousands of tourists could be streaming through the port, either embarking on a cruise or returning from one. For example, a Carnival Inspiration cruise is scheduled to arrive at the Port of Long Beach on March 28, 2014 (Cruisetimetables, 2012), which is the day after our scenario earthquake and a time when port infrastructure will be damaged and waterways will still be experiencing heightened currents. There is also a scheduled departure later that day for another Carnival Inspiration cruise, which has a maximum occupancy of 2,052 passengers and 920 onboard crew (Carnival, 2012). Thus, in addition to local residents and port employees dealing with the aftermath of the tsunami, there could be 5,000 more people attempting to come into the area, based on the 920 crew members, 2,052 people leaving the arriving cruise and 2,052 people boarding the departing ship.

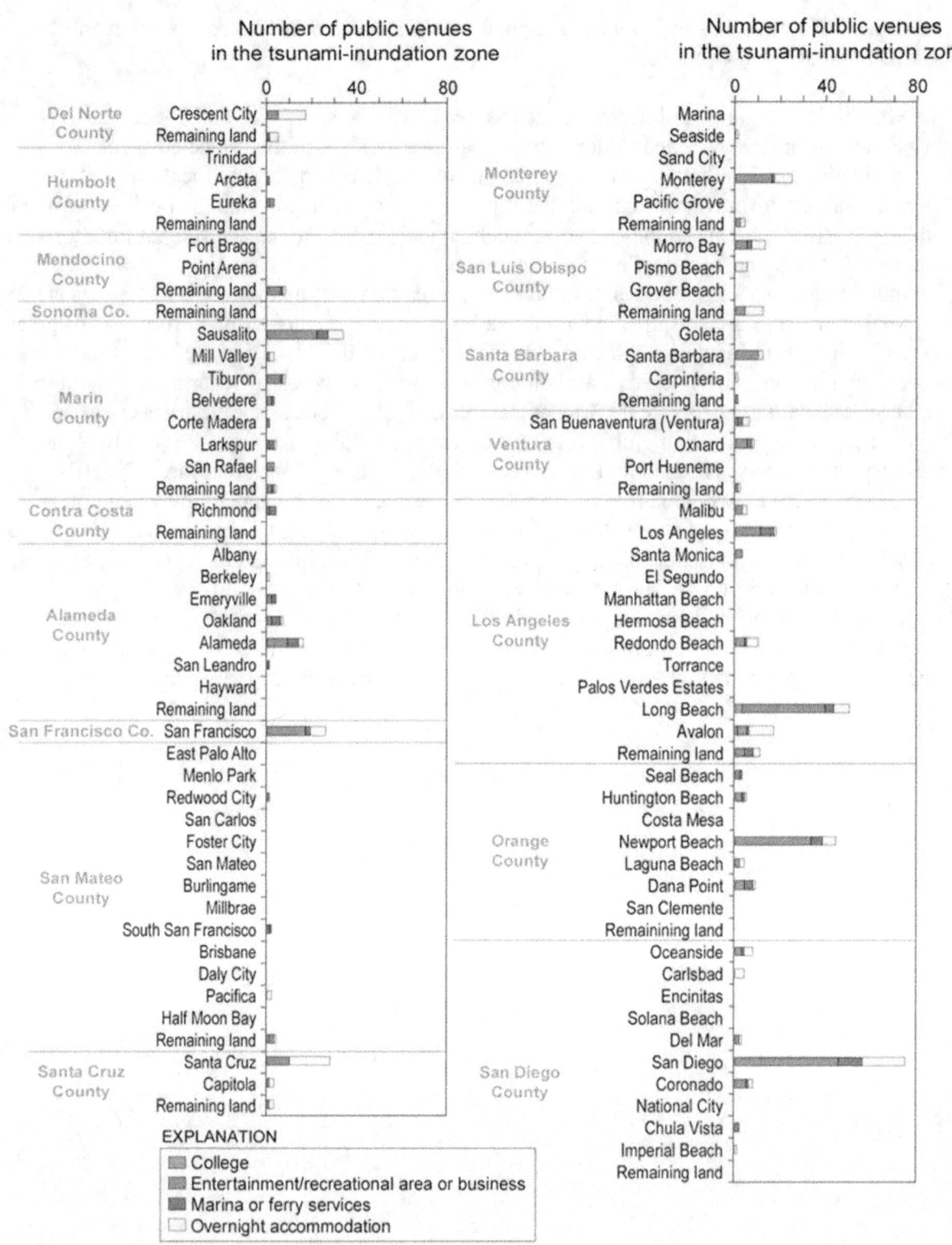

Figure 9. Plot showing number of public venues in the SAFRR scenario tsunami-inundation zone, California coast. Co., county.

Park and Beach Visitors

In addition to public venues, residents and tourists are drawn to the tsunami-inundation zone by the multiple recreational opportunities along the 1,200-mile California coastline (Visit California, 2012), including city, county, State, and national beaches, as well as parks and waterways. Estimating the magnitude of population exposure to tsunamis for these groups is difficult given their dynamic nature. The boating community is especially difficult given the large range of their locations throughout the day and the uncertainty of their points of entry to and departure from waterways. For example, sailboats in San Francisco Bay could have originated from nearby marinas in the bay or from marinas elsewhere, such as Half Moon Bay or other points on the West Coast. Because the California maritime community is vulnerable to even minor tsunamis, the State tsunami program is developing boater-preparedness information (California Geological Survey, 2012). Gauging the extent of maritime activity in coastal California waters is beyond the scope of this assessment, and subsequent discussion is limited to visitors to beaches and parks.

Analysis of visitor data from California's State parks (California State Parks, 2010) and national parks (National Park Service, 2011) indicates that 95 parks are in the scenario tsunami-inundation zone. For the 2009–2010 fiscal year, the average number of visitors to the 95 coastal parks was 60,707,359 people. This annual total equals 166,322 day-use visitors, on average, every day, assuming an equal distribution of visitors throughout the year. This average number of visitors is likely to be too low during the summer and on holidays, but too high for our scenario because of less favorable weather in March. National and State parks were coded by the primary county in which they are located to gauge the potential impact to communities. Although the State and national park visitors are outside of county jurisdictions, grouping the parks by county provides insight on where there may be significant tourist issues after a tsunami. When a National Oceanic and Atmospheric Administration (NOAA) tsunami alert is issued, adjacent county and city public-safety officials will be called on to evacuate populations at coastal parks. In addition to dealing with residents and employees during an evacuation, these counties may have to contend with a substantial number of visitors at nearby parks being directed into their jurisdictions.

Attendance numbers for city and county beaches were retrieved from the United States Lifesaving Association (USLA), where they are collected annually from beach lifeguards on a volunteer basis. Beach attendance is defined by the USLA as the "people recreating in the water or on the sand, and at adjacent picnic areas, parking lots, recreation concessions and bike paths…[but] does not include people that merely transit on bikes or in cars" (United States Lifesaving Association, 2012). Because estimates are provided by lifeguards on a volunteer basis, not all beaches on the California coast have data for every year, or at all in many cases. Data on annual beach attendance were compiled for 2010 and not 2011 because (1) 2010 data contained a greater number of beaches, and (2) 2010 beach data allows for comparisons with residential data from the 2010 census population count. This analysis yielded 27 beach jurisdictions that included city and county properties and were primarily in southern California (the city of Santa Cruz being the northern-most unit). Data was not available for beaches north of Santa Cruz, suggesting that the lifeguards there do not participate in the national data-collection effort or, more likely, that the smaller numbers of visitors to beaches in northern California do not merit government-supported lifeguard agencies (Kevin Miller, California Emergency Management Agency, oral commun., May 28, 2013).

Statistics on 2010 annual beach attendance indicate that California city and county beaches had 140,452,280 visitors, with the greatest number visiting beaches in Los Angeles County (59 million visitors) and San Diego (24 million visitors). Other beaches with high beach attendance are those in Long Beach (6.6 million), Huntington Beach (8.0 million), Newport Beach (7.1 million), Orange County (6.7 million), Laguna Beach (3.9 million), and Oceanside (3.8 million).

To translate annual numbers to estimates for this scenario, we relied on visitor-proportion values by Dwight and others (2007), who studied annual beach-attendance variability at 75 southern California beaches. Their work suggests that 5.2 percent of all visits occur in March, and 10 percent occur on a Thursday (with four Thursdays occurring in our scenario month). After accounting for this variability in beach attendance, and using these percentages, we estimate that 261,508 visitors would be at city, county, State, or Federal beaches and parks for our scenario tsunami on Thursday March 28, 2014 (fig. 10).

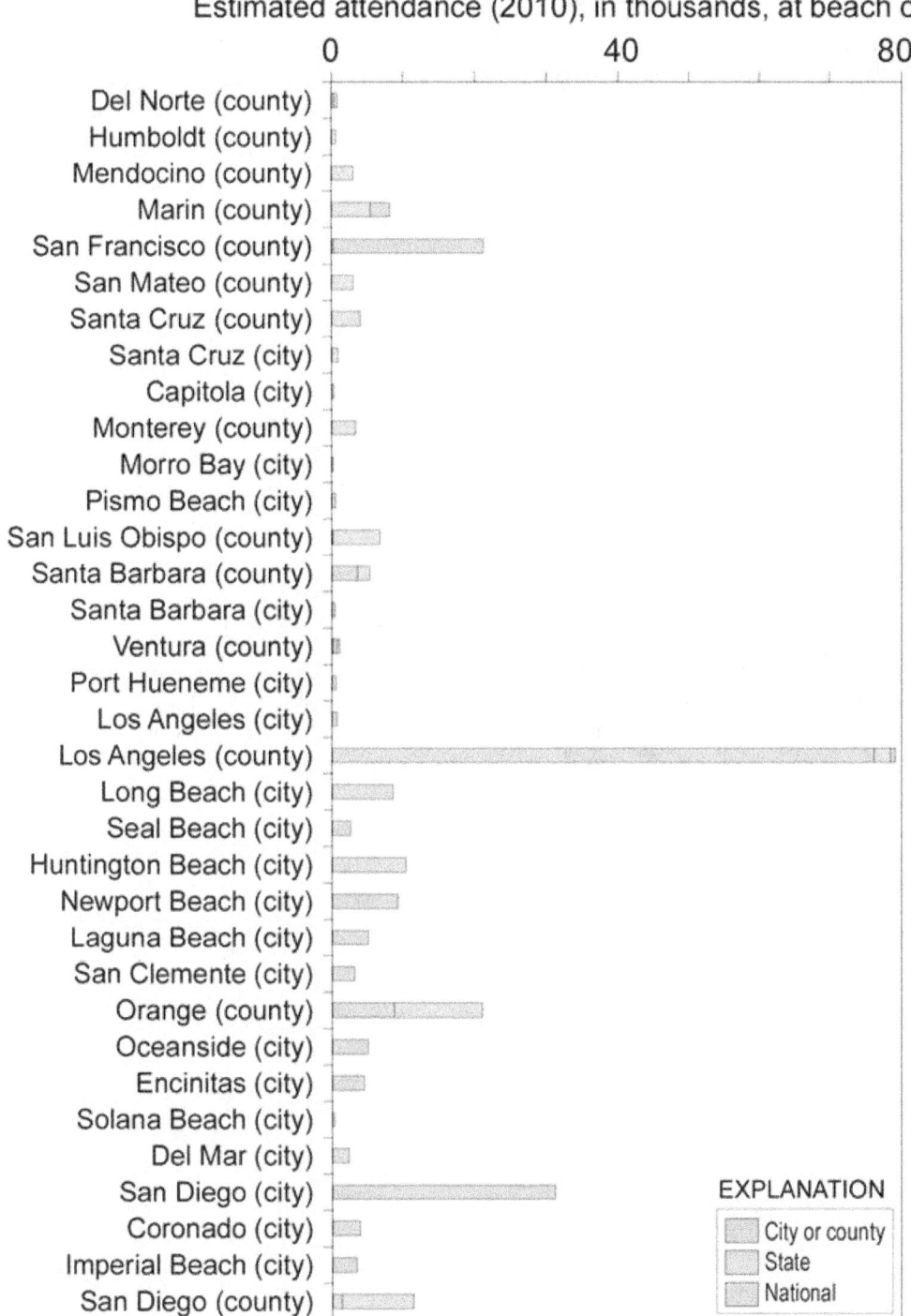

Figure 10. Plot showing estimated daily number of visitors ⸢in thousands⸥ for the SAFRR scenario to coastal California city and county beaches, State par⸢s, and ⸢ational Par⸢ Service locations grouped by city and county ⸢urisdictions.

Composite Index of Population Exposure

To provide a regional snap-shot of population exposure, we developed a composite index to compare community exposure to the SAFRR tsunami scenario for 95 geographic units—77 incorporated cities, 2 incorporated towns, and the remaining land in 16 counties[3]. The composite index was created by first normalizing values in each community for various population attributes to the maximum value in the category. Categories used for the index were the number of (1) residents, (2) employees, (3) public venues, (4) dependent-care facilities, (5) community-support businesses, and (6) beach and park visitors in the scenario tsunami-inundation zone. Normalizing data to maximum values creates a common data range of zero to one for all categories and is a simple approach for comparing disparate datasets. The normalized values in each community were added and, because there are six categories, the resulting scores ranged from zero to six (fig. 11). This unitless index allows us to compare the relative exposure levels for the 95 geographic units at regional or State levels. Because they are relative metrics, the numbers are meant for comparative purposes and do not provide much meaning for individual communities. In addition, this comparative index of population exposure simply reflects the magnitude of potential at-risk populations and does not incorporate the population density within a community, or potential limitations in egress options for evacuations.

Figure 11 illustrates the composite index for the 95 areas, where higher values indicate higher amounts. For example, the city of Long Beach has the highest composite amount value (4.6), indicating that this community consistently has one of the highest number of populations in the scenario tsunami-inundation zone. Other communities with high relative population exposure include Newport Beach, San Diego, San Francisco, and Sausalito. The dominant type of at-risk population varies somewhat in the cities and towns. For example, Long Beach has high relative exposure across all of the categories, except for beach and park attendance, whereas in Sausalito, population exposure is highest among employees, community-support businesses, and public venues.

---

[3] San Francisco is both a city and a county. Therefore, there are technically 17 counties in the scenario tsunami-inundation zone but we chose to discuss San Francisco as a city in the composite indices of population exposure and demographic sensitivity. This decision results in 16 counties for the comparative analysis.

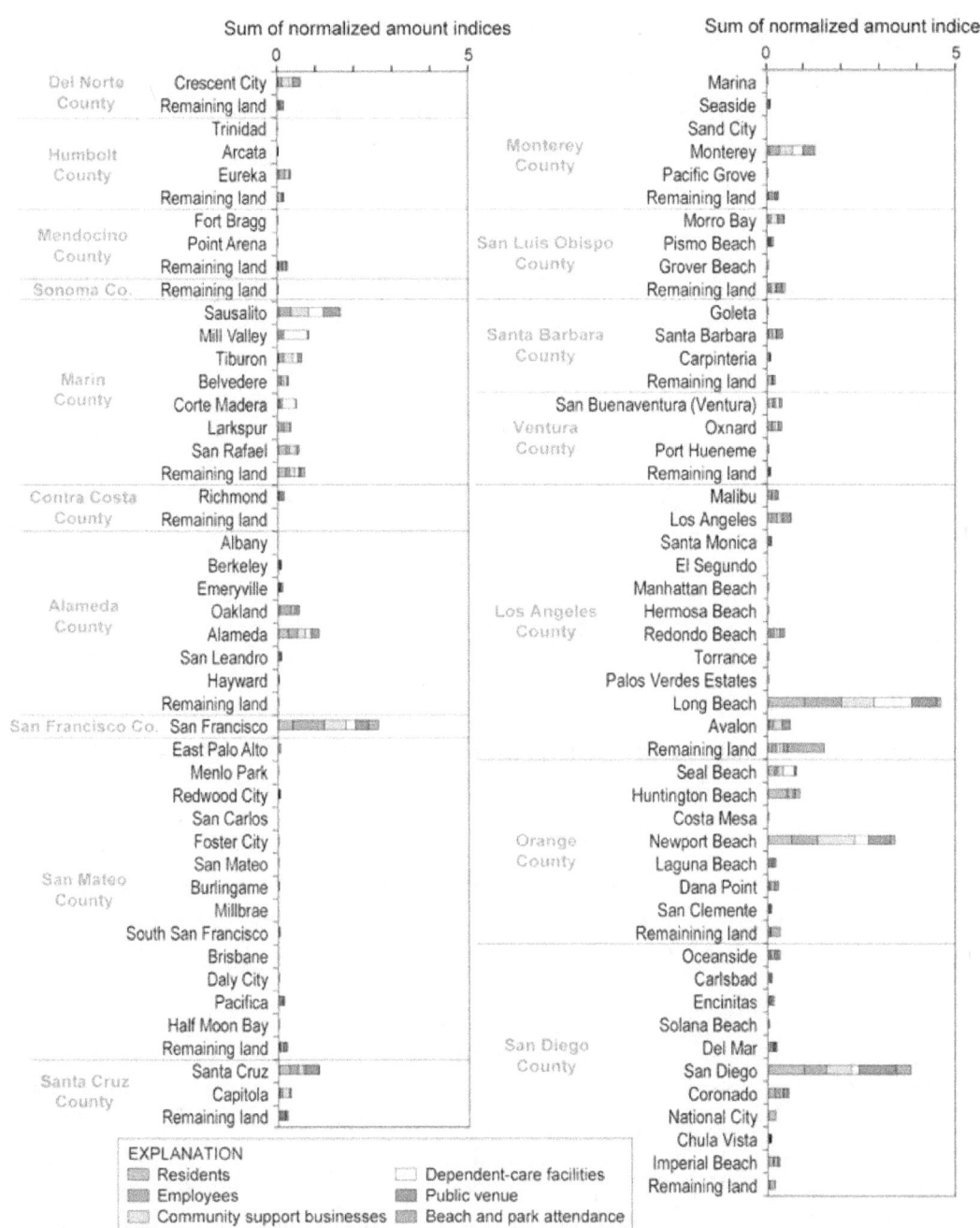

Figure 11. Plot comparing normalized amount indices for incorporated California cities and towns with land in the SAFRR scenario tsunami-inundation zone. Communities with the highest final scores have the highest numbers of residents, employees, community-support businesses, dependent-care facilities, public venues, and estimated beach and park visitors in the scenario tsunami-inundation zone. Although not observed, a final score of six would indicate that a community always had the highest number for each of the six categories.

Demographic Sensitivity to Evacuations

Demographic factors, such as age, ethnicity, and housing tenancy, can amplify an individual's sensitivity to hazards (Morrow, 1999; Cutter and others, 2003; Laska and Morrow, 2007; Ngo, 2003). In addition to general population counts, we calculated the number of residents in tsunami-prone areas based on census block-level data of ethnicity (Hispanic or Latino), race (American Indian and Alaska Native, Asian, Black or African American, Native Hawaiian and other Pacific Islander, and White—either for each race or in combination with one or more other races), age (individuals younger than 5 and older than 65 years in age), gender with particular family structures (female-headed households with children under 18 years of age and no spouse present), and housing tenancy (renter-occupied households). Categories to discuss demographic sensitivities are not based on extensive studies of residents in the scenario tsunami-inundation zone, but instead are based on past social-science research of all types of disasters (for example, earthquakes, tornadoes, and hurricanes). It is not implied that all individuals of a certain group will exhibit identical behavior. The extent of these demographic sensitivities will be influenced by variations in local physical and social context, level of preparedness before a tsunami, and ability to respond during an event (for example, access to a car for evacuation). Similar data are not available for employees or tourists, so our discussion of demographic sensitivity is limited to residential populations in the scenario tsunami-inundation zone.

Race and Ethnicity

Tsunami-warning and evacuation messages may be difficult for some at-risk individuals to understand and act upon because of language barriers. In the Los Angeles–Long Beach–Santa Ana metropolitan statistical area (MSA), approximately 14 percent of households are considered to be linguistically isolated, which means that no one age 14 or older speaks English "very well". Of those who are linguistically isolated, the primary languages spoken in households in the Los Angeles-Long Beach-Santa Ana MSA include Asian and Pacific Island languages (31 percent), Spanish (25 percent), other Indo-European languages (23 percent), or some other language (18 percent) (U.S. Census Bureau, 2010).

The distribution of populations with limited English skills is available in the U.S. Census Bureau's American Community Survey five-year estimates. However, the data are available only for census tracts, which are geographic units used by the U.S. Census Bureau to designate homogeneous subdivisions in counties and typically include between 1,500 and 8,000 people (U.S. Census Bureau, 2000). Because of the small spatial extent of potential inundation related to the SAFRR tsunami scenario and the much larger size of the census tracts, we determined that use of tract-level demographic data to describe characteristics of the population in the scenario-inundation zone could result in inaccurate conclusions (an example of ecological fallacy). We therefore decided to use only census data available at block level. Census blocks are the smallest geographic unit used by the U.S. Census Bureau; they often correspond to a city block and can range in population from none to several hundred people.

Because census blocks lack data on limited English skills, we cannot fully comment on demographic issues related to warning-message receipt. We do, however, examine race and ethnicity data that are available at the block level to provide some insight on potential language barriers, as well as any cultural differences in warning-message receipt and evacuation efforts. Our discussion of race and ethnicity and its relation to evacuation challenges for a distant-source tsunami is, however, a subset and simplification of how this topic is typically covered in the social science literature on societal risk, natural hazards, and disaster management. In this larger literature, race and ethnicity are treated in a broader context for their association with variations in socioeconomic status and access to resources that may constrain hazard preparedness, mitigation, response, and recovery (Mileti, 1999). Our discussion of race and ethnicity as a proxy for language or cultural barriers during tsunami evacuations, therefore, should be interpreted as preliminary comments to initiate community-level discussions and not as exhaustive or definitive statements on the topic.

One demographic group along the entire California coast that may warrant targeted tsunami education owing to potential language barriers or cultural differences is individuals that identify themselves as Hispanic or Latino. This problem was exhibited during the March 11, 2011, tsunami when Spanish-speaking residents over-evacuated many miles inland to the tops of coastal mountain ranges in several central coastal counties in California (Wilson and others, 2012). For the scenario tsunami, 15 percent of residents in the inundation zone consider themselves to be Hispanic or Latino. At the community level, the percentage of residents in the scenario inundation zone who are Hispanic or Latino ranges from 0 to 78 percent (city of San Rafael), and this percentage is high in other communities as well, such as East Palo Alto, Avalon, Seaside, and Santa Cruz (fig. 12).

With regard to differences in race, residents in the scenario tsunami-inundation zone identify themselves as White (81 percent), Black or African American (5 percent), Asian (10 percent), American Indian and Alaska Native (2 percent), and Native Hawaiian and Other Pacific Islander (less than 1 percent). Although the regional percentage is low for at-risk individuals who considered themselves to be Asian (10 percent), there is a substantial range of at-risk individuals at the community level from 0 to 74 percent (Hayward). Other communities with high Asian populations in the scenario inundation zone are in Alameda and San Mateo Counties, and include San Leandro, Daly City, Foster City, and Redwood City (fig. 13). As is the case regarding high concentrations of Hispanic or Latino populations, targeted outreach that acknowledges high concentrations of Asian populations may be warranted in some communities, such as evacuation messaging in multiple languages.

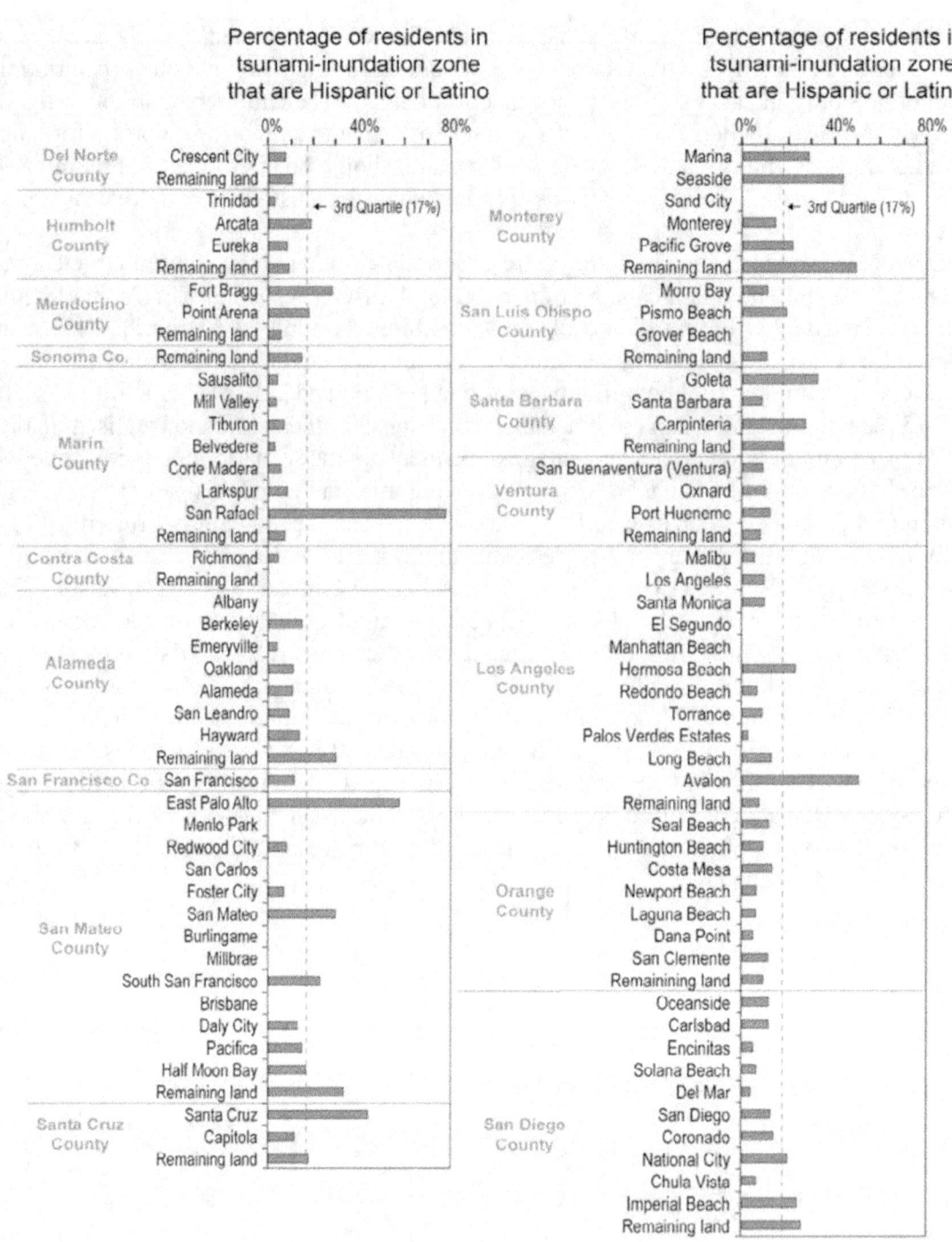

Figure 12. Plot showing percentage of residents in the California counties located in the SAFRR tsunami-inundation zone who identify themselves as ☐ispanic or ☐atino. Co., county.

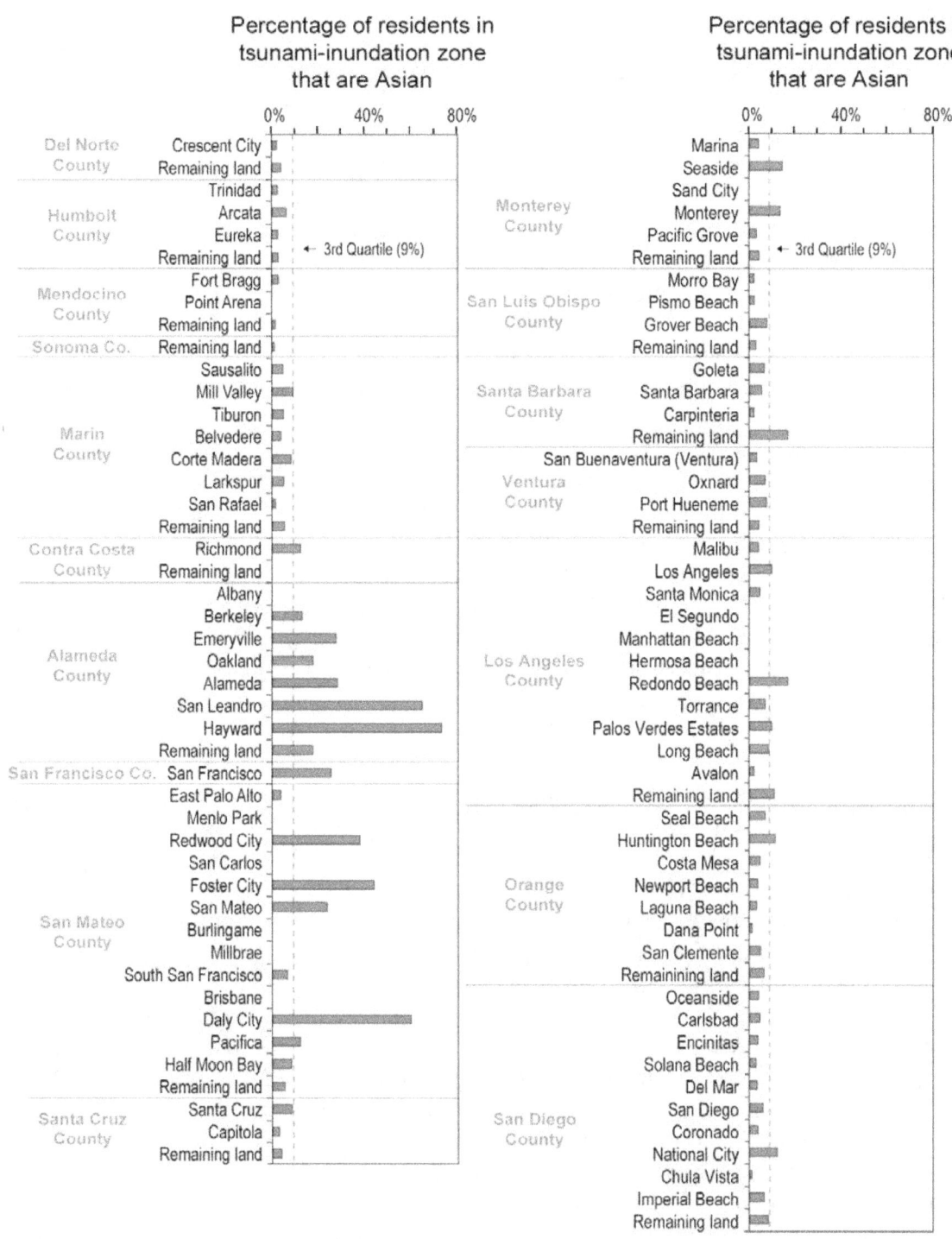

Figure 13. Plot showing percentage of residents in the California counties located in the SAFRR tsunami-inundation zone who identify themselves as Asian [either alone or in combination with other races]. Co., county.

Age

The very young and very old are considered to be more vulnerable than other age groups to sudden-onset hazards because of potential mobility and health issues (Morrow, 1999; Balaban, 2006; McGuire and others, 2007; Ngo, 2003). The very young (defined here as individuals less than 5 years in age) are considered to have heightened vulnerability because they often require direction and assistance to evacuate owing to their immaturity and size. They are also prone to developing post-traumatic stress disorders, depression, anxieties, and behavioral disorders as a result of their inability to comprehend and process the effects of a disaster (Balaban, 2006). Individuals less than 5 years in age represent a small percentage of residents in the scenario tsunami-inundation zone, specifically 4 percent across the State as a whole, and a typical range of 0 to 5 percent within individual communities[4]. Because of the low values and the small range in values among communities, we do not provide a bar graph to compare communities; however, data for individual communities are available for those interested.

The first tsunami wave of the SAFRR scenario is predicted to arrive on a Thursday afternoon; therefore, most children will be at school or at daycare centers. Schools often have evacuation plans, but like hospitals, rarely fully exercise them. Schools will have practiced vacating the building because of fire drills, but they may not know how to move students away from the school. Because there will be more than 4 hours between tsunami warning and arrival, school officials may dismiss students and staff before the tsunami is predicted to occur. This situation may add to the existing challenge of evacuating all residents safely because increased traffic will likely impede evacuation or school buses may not be readily available for people who need to evacuate. For example, other schools near, but outside of, the tsunami-inundation zone may be used for evacuation sites, which could further complicate evacuations (Rick Wilson, California Geological Survey, oral commun., May 28, 2013). Daycare centers for younger children also may have evacuation challenges. These centers are often private businesses and may not be included in official warning protocols of emergency personnel. They may not have a system in place to receive official warnings, are unlikely to have a television or radio on, and therefore, may not receive warnings in a timely manner. These centers are unlikely to have the capacity to transport multiple small children away from the tsunami-inundation zone and would most likely depend upon parents coming to the site to retrieve the children. As discussed earlier, parents may have difficulty getting to daycare centers if evacuation traffic clogs the roads.

The distribution of individuals older than 65 years has greater variability across the study area. This population is considered to have heightened vulnerability due to decreased mobility and health issues, reluctance to evacuate, the need for special medical equipment at shelters (McGuire and others, 2007), and the lack of social and economic resources to recover (Morrow, 1999; Ngo, 2003). Individuals older than 65 years represent 15 percent of all residents in the tsunami-inundation zone for the State as a whole, with a range from 0 to 44 percent (Mill Valley) within individual communities (fig. 14). The high percentages of at-risk individuals who are more than 65 years in age in Manhattan Beach, Pacific Grove, and Chula Vista, are due to a low number of residents in the tsunami-inundation zone (1, 2, and 6 residents, respectively). For those communities with large elderly populations in the inundation zone, unique evacuation procedures and sheltering protocols may be warranted.

---

[4] Approximately 20 percent of residents in the scenario tsunami-inundation zone of unincorporated San Diego County are less than 5 years in age. This higher percentage is because of the low number of total residents in the tsunami-inundation zone (247 residents) and does not reflect the regional trend.

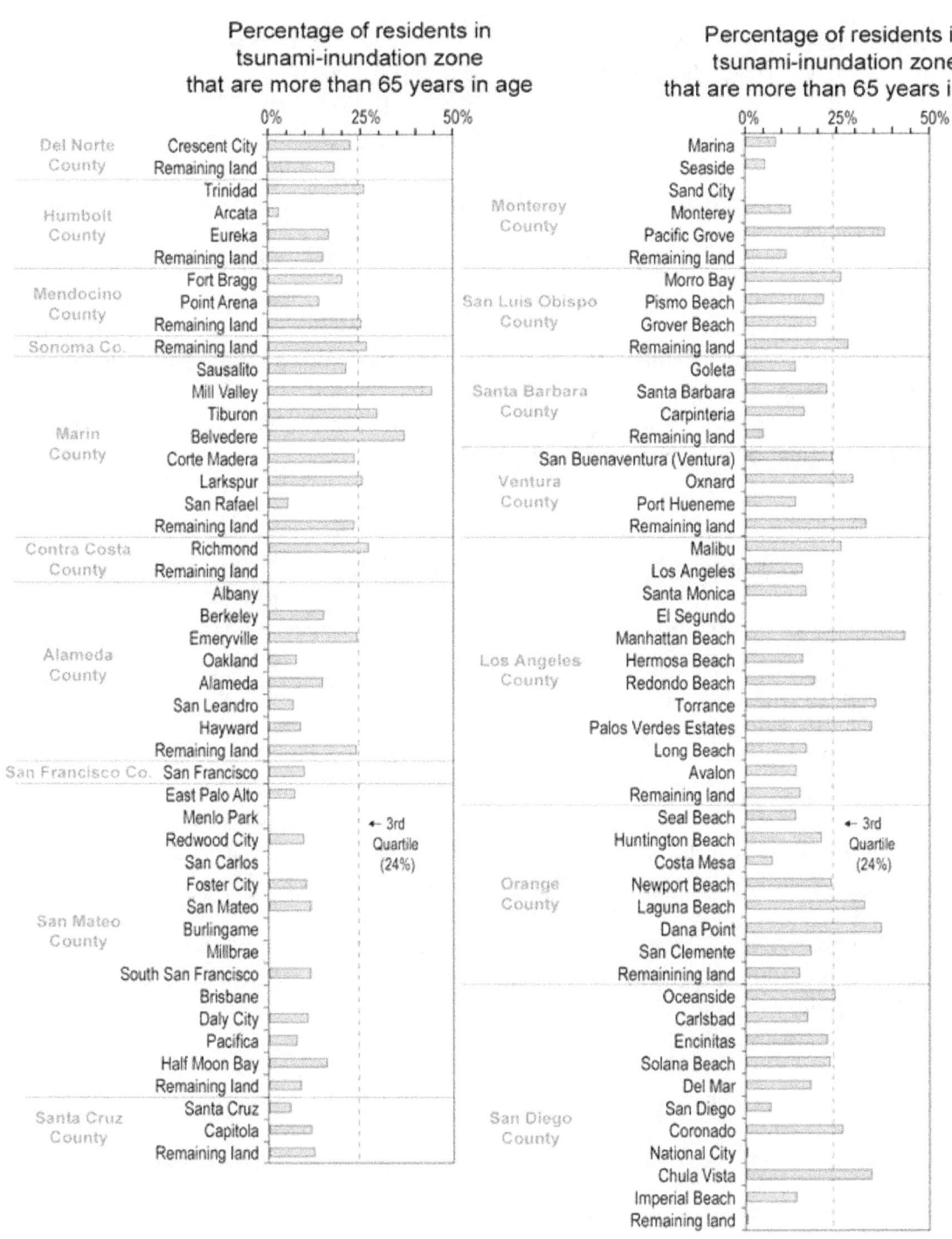

Figure 14. Plot showing percentage of residents in the California counties located in the SAFRR tsunami-inundation zone who are more than ☐☐ years old. Co., county.

Family Structure

Female-headed households with children under the age of 18 and no spouse present (that is, single-mother households) may be more vulnerable to future tsunamis than other households because of potential mobility issues during an evacuation and fewer financial resources to draw on when preparing for natural hazards and recovering from disasters (Enarson and Morrow, 1998; Laska and Morrow, 2007). Approximately 4 percent of households in the scenario tsunami-inundation zone are single-mother households. The highest percentages of households in the tsunami-inundation zone that are female-headed, have children under the age of 18, and have no spouse present are in Berkeley (17 percent), East Palo Alto (16 percent) and Arcata (14 percent). The high percentages of single-mother households in these communities are due to a low number of households in the tsunami-inundation zone (8, 197, and 64 households, respectively), which is apparent in the low third-quartile value of 5 single-mother households among communities in the tsunami-inundation zone. Because of the low values and the small range in values among communities, we do not provide a bar graph to compare communities; however, data for individual communities is available for those who are interested.

Housing Tenancy

Another group considered more vulnerable to and less prepared for extreme natural hazard events is renters (Morrow, 1999; Burby and others, 2003). This lack of preparation may result from (1) higher turnover rates for renters may limit their exposure to outreach efforts, (2) preparedness campaigns may pay less attention to renters, (3) renters typically have lower incomes and fewer resources to recover, and (4) renters may not be motivated to invest in mitigation measures for rented property (Burby and others, 2003). After a disaster, renters also have little control over the speed with which rental housing is repaired or replaced (Laska and Morrow, 2007).

Approximately 53 percent of the occupied housing units in the scenario tsunami-inundation zone for the State as a whole are renter occupied. This ranges from 0 percent in some communities up to 100 percent in others (fig. 15), although high values in many communities reflect a small total number of occupied households in the tsunami-inundation zone, such as Costa Mesa, Manhattan Beach, Port Hueneme, and the unincorporated parts of San Diego County (10, 1, 6, and 76 households, respectively). For many of the remaining communities, renter-occupied households represent the majority of households in the tsunami-inundation zone. In the top 25 percent of the at-risk communities, renter-occupied households constitute at least 60 percent of the households.

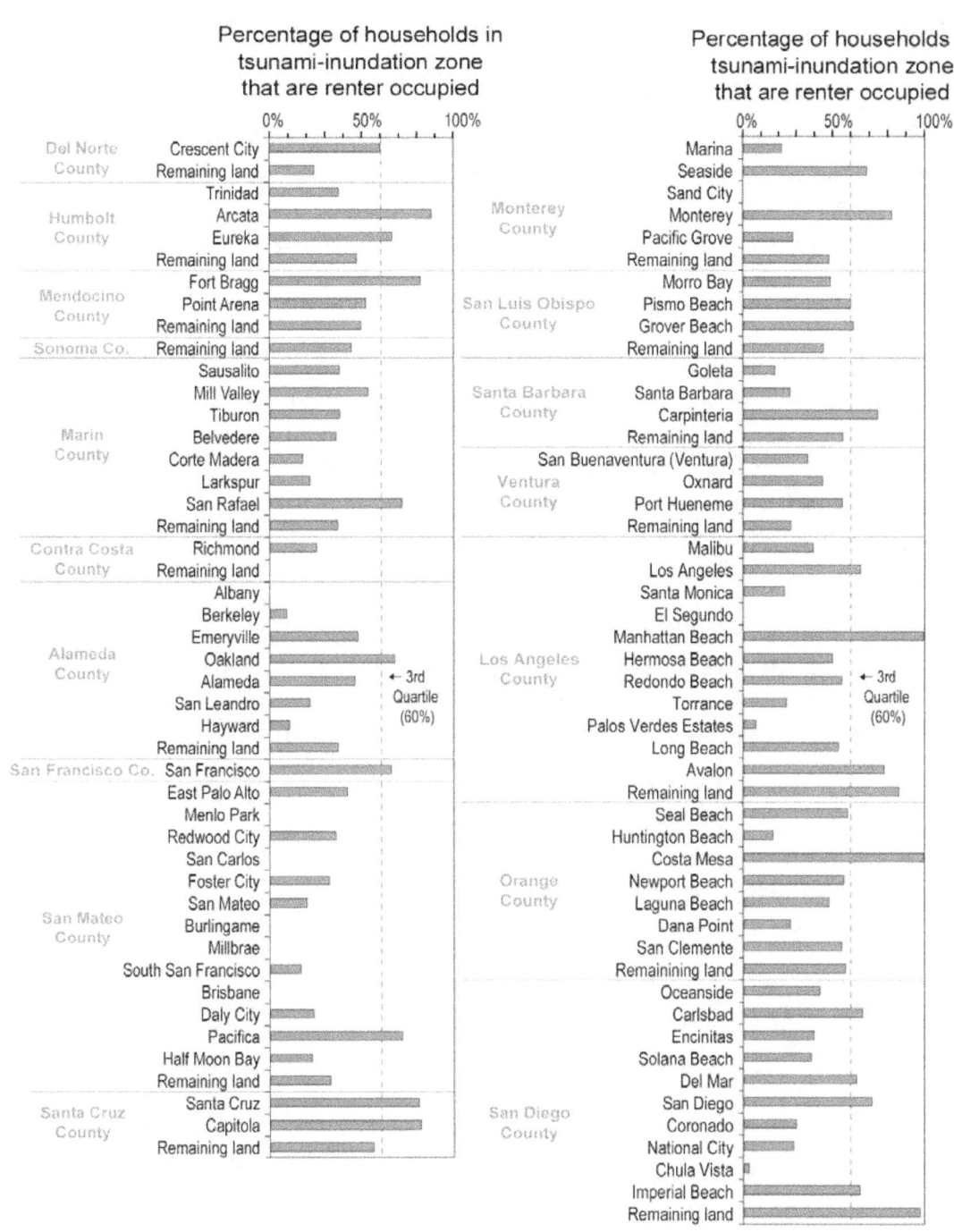

Figure 15. Plot showing percentage of households in the California counties located in the SAFRR scenario tsunami-inundation zone that are renter occupied. Co., county.

Group Quarters

Another group of residents who will require special attention during and before a tsunami are those in group quarters, either institutionalized (for example, adult correctional, juvenile correctional, and nursing facilities) or noninstitutionalized (for example, college/university student housing and military quarters) (fig. 16). The SAFRR scenario tsunami-inundation zone contains 199 residents in institutionalized group quarters, with most of them in Alameda, San Diego, Mill Valley, and Santa Cruz (51, 43, 37, and 35 residents, respectively). Where these institutionalized populations do exist in the tsunami-inundation zone, emergency managers and public-safety officials may need to develop structured evacuations and continued supervision to ensure the safety of both the institutionalized populace and the neighboring communities. Because of the low values and the small range in values among communities, we do not provide a bar graph to compare communities; however, data for individual communities are available for those who are interested.

Some correctional institutions, such as Federal Correctional Institution on Terminal Island near the Port of Los Angeles and San Quentin State Prison in Marin County, are close to the landward extent of predicted tsunami inundation for this scenario, but not technically in the inundation zone. However, emergency managers still may decide to call for evacuations from these facilities given the uncertainty inherent in the tsunami modeling and local landscape conditions, the need to have sufficient time to evacuate before they receive full knowledge of the event, and the consequences of not evacuating these facilities.

There are 9,911 residents in the SAFRR tsunami-inundation zone that are in noninstitutionalized group quarters (fig. 16). Approximately 82 percent of this population is in San Diego (5,544 residents), Coronado (231 residents), and National City (2,342 residents), all likely reflecting military quarters associated with the naval bases near those communities. Warning these populations may be challenging to local officials because the at-risk population may not be familiar with local hazard issues, may not have experienced or have knowledge of past disasters in the area, and may not have been exposed to tsunami-awareness efforts if such efforts are geared for homeowners. There also may be military evacuation protocols that may or may not reflect local emergency-management plans.

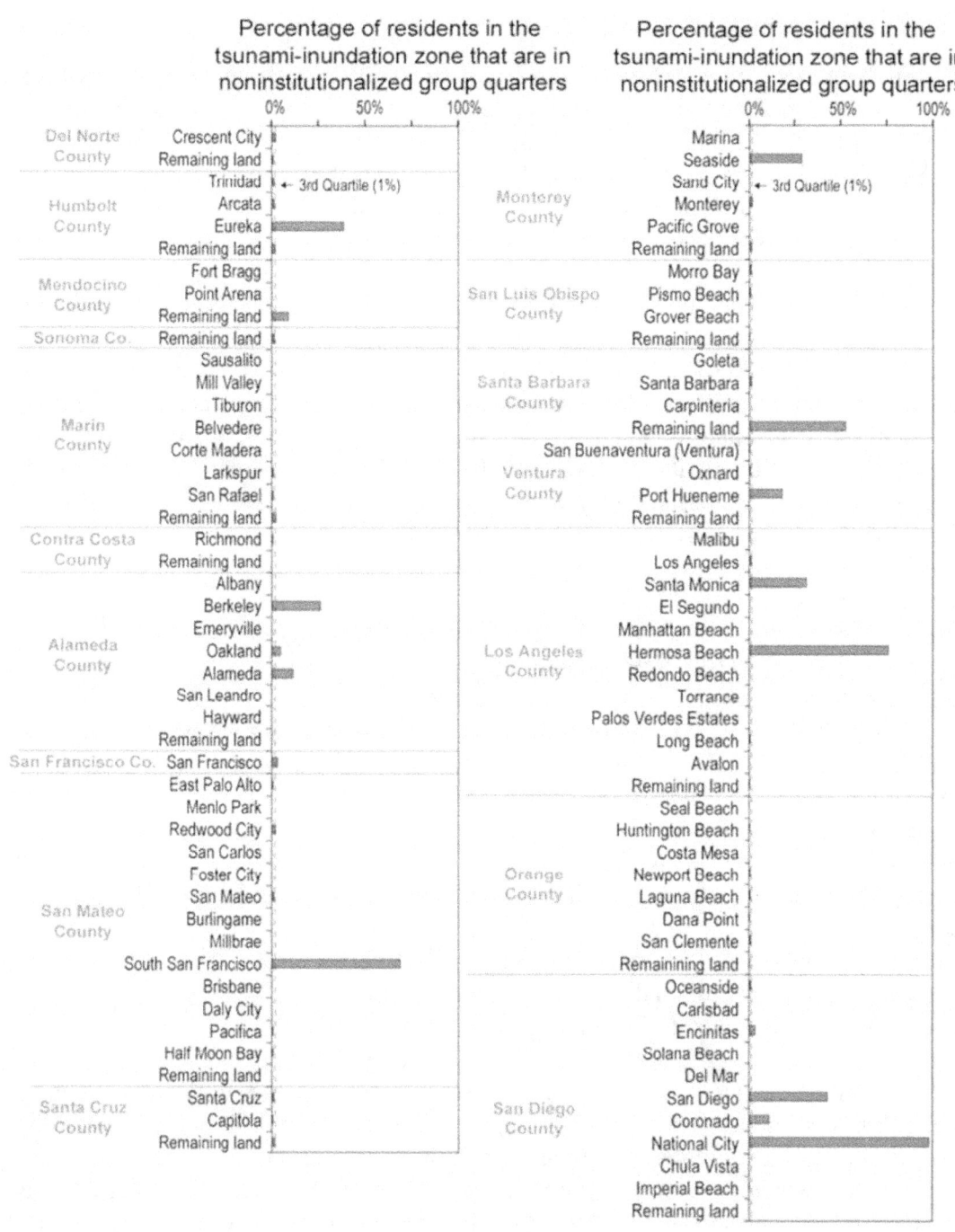

Figure 16. Plot showing percentage of residents in the California counties located in the SAFRR tsunami-inundation zone who are in noninstitutionalized group quarters. Co., county.

Composite Index of Population Sensitivity

Throughout this section, we have highlighted various demographic attributes that may make preparing for and responding to tsunamis more challenging for at-risk residents. Parsing out individual demographic attributes provides some insight in evacuation challenges, but it is somewhat simplistic because individuals and the communities they live in are not one-dimensional. For example, renters, small children, and or non-English-speaking residents all present evacuation challenges on their own and these difficulties are compounded when all three attributes are found in the same neighborhood.

To provide some insight on the multidimensional nature of the neighborhoods in the SAFRR tsunami-inundation zone, we developed a composite index similar to the one described earlier for population exposure. We again compared the 77 incorporated cities, 2 incorporated towns and the remaining land in the 16 counties by normalizing values in each community for various demographic attributes to the maximum value in the category and then added these normalized values to yield a final aggregated number. For this composite index, we focused on the percentages of residents (or households in some cases) in the SAFRR scenario tsunami-inundation zone of each community who are in the following categories:

- Hispanic or Latino,
- Black or African American (either alone or in combination with other races),
- American Indian and Alaska Native (either alone or in combination with other races),
- Asian (either alone or in combination with other races),
- Native Hawaiian and other Pacific Islander (either alone or in combination with other races),
- Some Other Race (other than White, Black or African American, American Indian and Alaska Native, Asian, or Native Hawaiian and other Pacific Islander),
- Residents less than 5 years in age,
- Residents more than 65 years in age,
- Occupied households that are female-headed with children under the age of 18 and no spouse present,
- Occupied households that are renter occupied,
- Residents that are in institutionalized group quarters, and
- Residents that are in noninstitutionalized group quarters.

These attributes of block-level census data were chosen because of potential language barriers or cultural differences (race and ethnicity attributes), mobility issues (age and family structure attributes and institutionalized populations), or potential issues in warning dissemination (group quarters and renters) that may influence the ability of at-risk individuals to effectively receive or respond to a tsunami warning. Our previous discussion of these various demographic attributes is a subset of how these attributes are typically covered in the social-science literature on societal risk and natural hazards. This simple composite index of demographic sensitivity should be interpreted as preliminary comments to initiate community-level discussions on the types of people that are in tsunami-inundation zones and not as exhaustive or definitive statements on any one demographic attribute.

Figure 17 illustrates variations in the composite demographic-sensitivity index for the 95 areas, where higher values indicate higher sensitivity. Although not observed, a final score of 12 would indicate that one community always had the highest percentage in each of the 12 categories. The city of East Palo Alto has the highest sensitivity value (5.4), indicating that this community consistently has high percentages of residents in several of the demographic categories. Other communities with high relative sensitivity include San Rafael, San Mateo, Fort Bragg, and Arcata, as well as the unincorporated parts of San Diego County.

Various reasons lead to high values for different communities. Of the 95 geographic units, 19 have high relative values (we chose a normalized value of 0.66 or higher) in 1 category, 10 units have high values in 2 categories, San Rafael has high values in 3 categories, and East Palo Alto has high values in 4 categories. The high composite sensitivity value in East Palo Alto (5.4) is primarily due to the high percentages of residents who identify themselves as Hispanic or Latino, Native Hawaiian and other Pacific Islander, and some other race, and as single-mother households. In unincorporated San Diego County (4.2), higher sensitivity values are because of high percentages of residents who are less than 5 years in age; in San Rafael (4.0), the higher values result from high percentages of residents who identify themselves as Hispanic or Latino, some other race, and as renter-occupied households. In Fort Bragg and Arcata (both 3.4), higher sensitivity values are the result of high percentages of households that are occupied by renters or by single mothers.

The primary point of this exercise is to demonstrate that the type of residents in the SAFRR tsunami-inundation zone is not consistent among the at-risk communities and counties; therefore, general tsunami education and preparedness efforts that do not address local conditions or needs may not be as effective as those that do target efforts. Tsunami warning and education efforts may need to reflect a mix of certain language or cultural issues in one community, but acknowledge a mix of renters and children in another community.

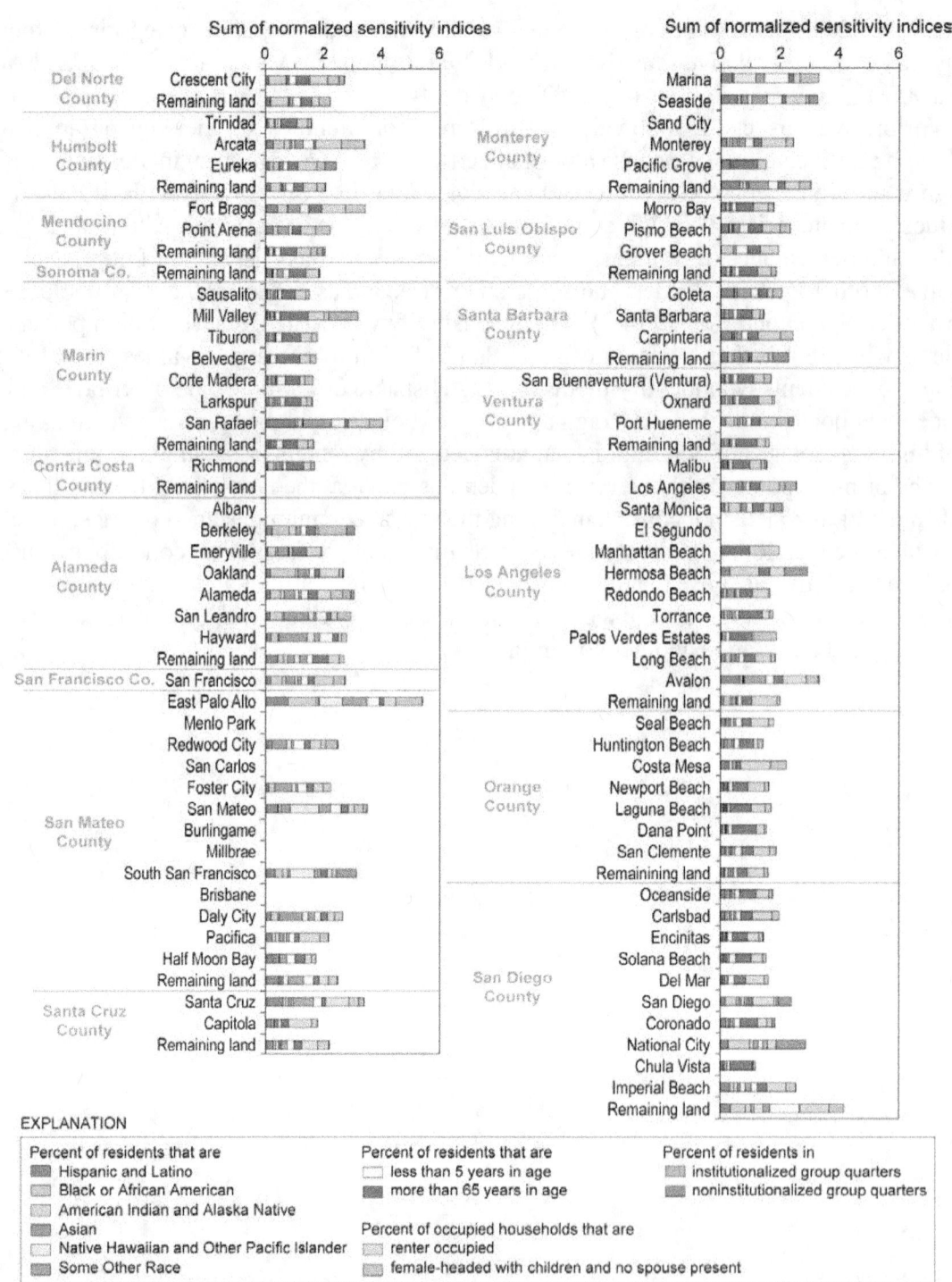

Figure 17. Plot comparing normalized demographic-sensitivity indices for incorporated cities and towns for California counties with land in the SAFRR tsunami-inundation zone. Communities with the highest final scores have the highest percentages of various demographic attributes that suggest greater sensitivity to preparing for and responding to e□treme events. Co., county.

Magnitude and Challenges of Tsunami Evacuations

When tsunamis occur, emergency managers do not have the luxury of knowing which areas will flood prior to calling for evacuations. Instead, they must make evacuation decisions based on existing knowledge of potential tsunami-inundation zones, discussions with representatives of the NOAA tsunami-warning centers and other emergency managers, and their own level of risk tolerance. To help this process and to support other tsunami risk-reduction efforts in California, a set of statewide tsunami-inundation maps have been developed and released by the California Tsunami Hazard Mitigation and Preparation Program, which is a collaboration of the California Geological Survey and the California Emergency Management Agency (California Geological Survey, 2012). These maps were created for the most significant population and economic centers on the California coast and are based on cumulative modeling efforts that incorporate a variety of large distant-source and local tsunamigenic earthquake scenarios and local landslide sources that can also generate tsunamis.

If the SAFRR scenario tsunami were to occur, emergency managers would likely use the statewide tsunami-inundation zone, or their own local evacuation zones, which are more conservative, to determine which areas to evacuate. To provide some insight on how well the statewide zone reflects potential inundation from our scenario event, we compared the number of residents in the two different zones and report results at the community level (fig. 18). Results are cumulative in figure 18; therefore, the total number of residents in the scenario inundation zone is shown in blue, and the total number of residents in the maximum tsunami-zone is the sum of the blue and orange bars. The statewide maximum tsunami-inundation zone was mapped for a slightly greater area than the SAFRR tsunami scenario. This is not an issue in the communities listed in figure 18, which are included in both mapping efforts, but may slightly affect comparisons of estimates for the unincorporated portions of each county (noted as "remaining land").

The scenario tsunami-inundation zone contains approximately 91,956 residents, who represent 34 percent of the estimated 267,381 residents in the statewide maximum tsunami-inundation zone (Wood and others, 2012). In most communities, such as Emeryville, Alameda, Oakland, Oxnard, Los Angeles, and Huntington Beach (fig. 18), residential exposure in the scenario inundation zone is substantially smaller than that for the maximum tsunami-inundation zone. In these communities, evacuations for our scenario event would require more residents than necessary to leave their homes. This should not be considered an "over-evacuation" because more precise information is not available, and real-time tsunami-inundation modeling is not currently operational at NOAA tsunami-warning centers. However, emergency managers in these communities should be prepared to communicate why the extensive evacuations were taken, namely the interest in saving lives, low-risk tolerance for responding to the event, the lack of more-precise inundation areas, and the inherent uncertainty of tsunami generation, propagation, and inundation. These moments, which were once communicated as false alarms, provide outreach opportunities to discuss tsunami science, monitoring, and preparedness. There are several communities, such as Long Beach and San Diego, where the scenario event is a close approximation of the statewide tsunami-inundation zone. In 26 of the communities in our analysis, resident exposure to the scenario inundation zone is 75 percent or more, which is equal to the exposure to the maximum tsunami-inundation zone. In these communities, emergency managers will be able to leverage any preexisting public outreach or training that has occurred in relation to the maximum tsunami-inundation zones. Results also show that although the scenario tsunami is not the primary tsunami threat to most California coastal communities, it is a substantial threat to several communities, particularly in southern California.

This comparison demonstrates the utility of having tsunami-scenario catalogs prior to events to help guide evacuation decisionmaking (for example, Wilson and Miller, 2012), instead of only relying on maximum tsunami-inundation zones. It also demonstrates the utility of real-time inundation modeling during actual events, such as the Short-term Inundation Forecasting for Tsunamis (SIFT) system currently under development for operational use in NOAA Tsunami Warning Centers (Titov and others, 2001).

Evacuations may be particularly difficult in areas with limited egress options, such as island and peninsula communities. If all at-risk individuals on an island attempt to evacuate by car, then traffic congestion is likely, and even a four-hour evacuation window before wave arrival (6 hours in southern California) for the USGS tsunami scenario may be inadequate. To illustrate this issue, figure 19 shows a collection of islands in Newport Beach with substantial residential populations, several of which have thousands of residents in areas where egress to the mainland is limited to one road, such as Balboa Island and Lido Isle (2,756 and 1,626 residents, respectively). In addition, more than 8,000 residents would also be asked to evacuate Balboa peninsula because it is completely within the statewide maximum tsunami-inundation zone.

In addition, more than 8,000 residents would also be asked to evacuate Balboa peninsula because it is completely within the statewide maximum tsunami-inundation zone. To date, we are not aware of any traffic studies for Balboa peninsula or the other islands in the Newport Beach area to determine the amount of time necessary for complete evacuations; therefore, it is unclear how long it would take to evacuate these areas in response to the USGS tsunami scenario (Anthony Brine, City of Newport Beach Public Works Department, oral commun., February 12, 2013). Although it was beyond the scope of this scenario assessment, an analysis of time requirements for complete evacuations may be warranted to assist with future tsunami-response planning efforts.

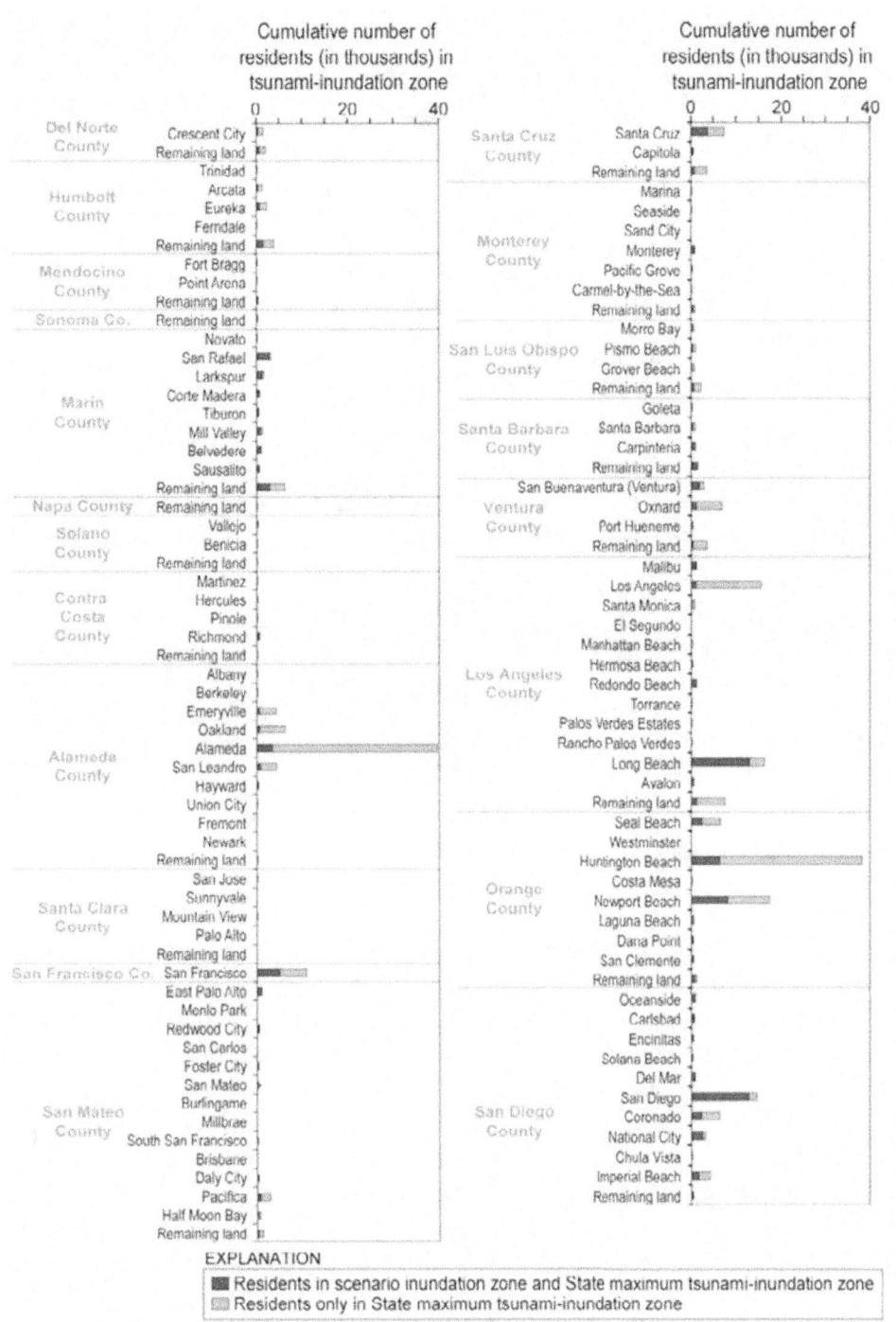

Figure 18. Plot showing cumulative number of residents in the SAFRR tsunami scenario and California tsunami-inundation zones. Co., county.

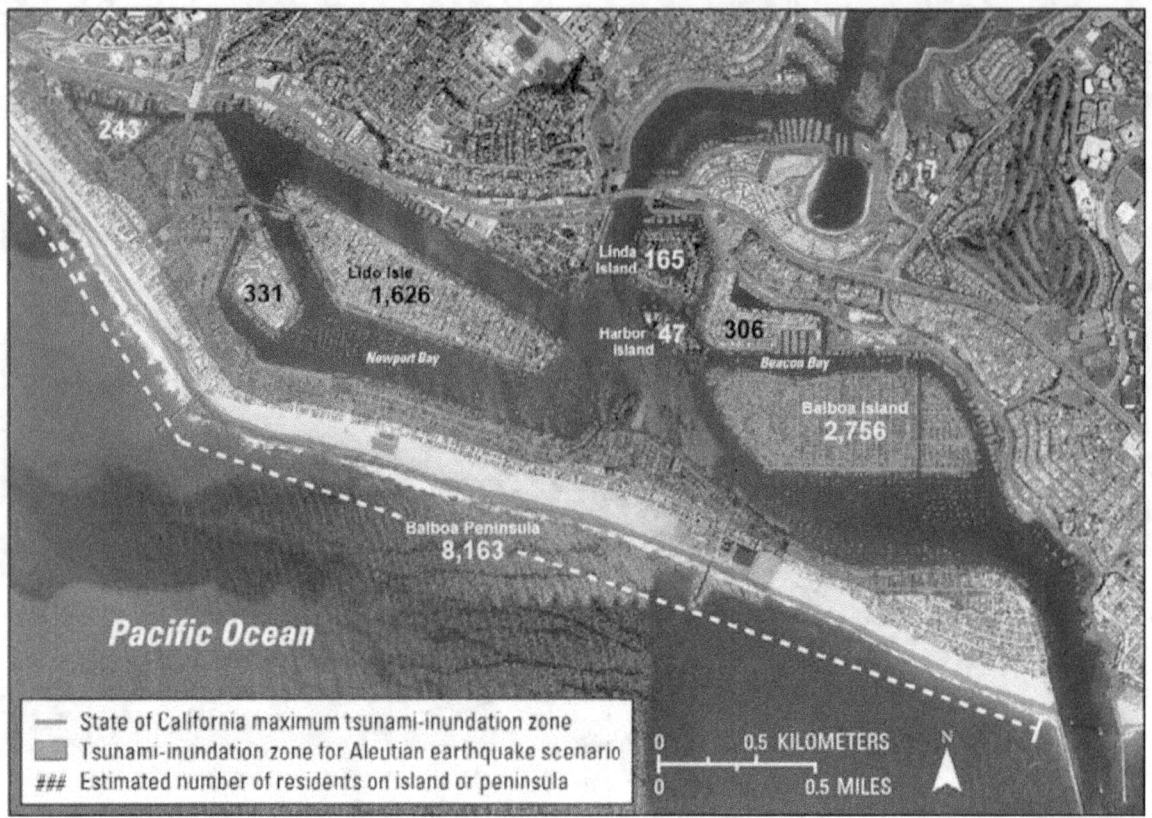

Figure 19. Photograph showing inundation zones for the SAFRR tsunami scenario and the statewide maximum zone, as well as estimated residential population counts [based on 2010 U.S. Census Bureau data] for island communities in Newport Beach, California.

The Newport Beach collection of islands also bolsters the case for scenario-specific evacuation maps instead of a maximum tsunami-inundation zone that drives evacuation decisionmaking. In this study area, scenario-specific inundation maps may reduce the likelihood of potentially unnecessary complete evacuations of Balboa Peninsula, Lido Isle, Linda Island, and Harbor Island, where the maximum inundation zones cover the locations entirely, but the scenario zone does not. In each of these areas, at-risk populations would have areas on the islands or the peninsula that are outside of likely inundation from the SAFRR tsunami scenario.

The islands and peninsula within Newport Beach are not the only places where evacuations may be challenging because of limited egress options and substantial populations on islands. We highlighted the Newport Beach area to illustrate the issue of island communities simply because of the high concentration of islands in this area. Other areas along the California coast with potential tsunami-evacuation challenges that may warrant discussions between emergency managers and traffic engineers include

· Treasure Island in San Francisco (2,880 residents);
· Bay Farm and Alameda Islands in Alameda (12,588 and 60,212 residents, respectively);
· Naples Island and Alamitos Park Peninsula in Long Beach (3,435 and 1,448 residents, respectively);
· Seabridge (1,053 residents), Sunset Beach (3,378 residents), Trinidad Island (881 residents), Humboldt Island (784 residents), and Davenport Island (511 residents) in Huntington Beach;

44

- Mission Beach in San Diego (4,700 residents); and
- Silver Strand Boulevard connecting the City of Coronado peninsula to the mainland (4,799 residents).

Sheltering Requirements

The scenario tsunami could damage many homes along the California coast, forcing some residents to find shelter in the short term. Residents could also be displaced because of lack of access due to flooded roadways or because of long-term disruption damage to services (for example, water, wastewater, or electricity). Some residents may have friends and family to help them out, and others may have the financial resources to afford temporary housing or to move. Some people, however, may need to rely on publicly provided shelters, at least in the short term, while damaged homes are repaired. To gauge the potential sheltering needs in the aftermath of the scenario tsunami, we used equations contained in the Hazus-MH 2.1 flood loss-estimation methodology (Federal Emergency Management Agency, 2013).

Estimated sheltering needs are based on the magnitude of the displaced population and then modified by their income levels and age distributions. Individuals with lower incomes will be more likely to use publicly provided shelters. Age also plays a role, where younger, less established families and elderly families will be more likely to use shelters. A full description of the method of estimating sheltering needs can be found in appendix A.

Analysis was completed with population-count and age-distribution data available at the census-block level. Income distributions are available for census block groups; therefore, income-distribution values were assigned to each block based on the larger block group value. Because of the small area likely to be inundated by the scenario tsunami, estimating sheltering needs at the census block was considered more accurate than the block group. The displaced population based on block-group-level data is 128,906 residents, which is 40 percent higher than the value using block-level data. Calculation errors in sheltering needs, therefore, could be off by 40 percent of the actual value if we used data at the block group level. We decided assigning block-group-level income distributions to census-block boundaries would result in fewer errors than using block-group boundaries with associated data on total residents and age distributions.

Based on the number of estimated residents in the tsunami-inundation zone and their age and income distributions, we estimate 8,678 individuals may require publicly provided shelters after the scenario tsunami (fig. 20). This number reflects 9 percent of the estimated number of residents in the scenario tsunami-inundation zone. The low percentage is likely a reflection of the typically higher incomes for households along the California coast. The communities with the highest number of people with sheltering needs include San Diego (1,095 residents), Long Beach (1,060 residents), Newport Beach (711 residents), Santa Cruz (522 residents), and National City (498 residents). Sheltering needs in National City likely will be provided by the military, rather than by city or county organizations, because 99 percent of the at-risk residents in that community are in noninstitutionalized group quarters which include military quarters. High resident demand for public shelters after the scenario tsunami may occur in San Diego (2,121 residents), Orange (1,482 residents), Los Angeles (1,418 residents), and Marin (876 residents) Counties. The length of time displaced people may need publicly provided shelters is unknown because estimating the extent of damage to individual homes is beyond the scope of this project. Some people may evacuate to shelters while tsunami waves are arriving during the predicted 12 or more hours, but then return to their homes after the event.

45

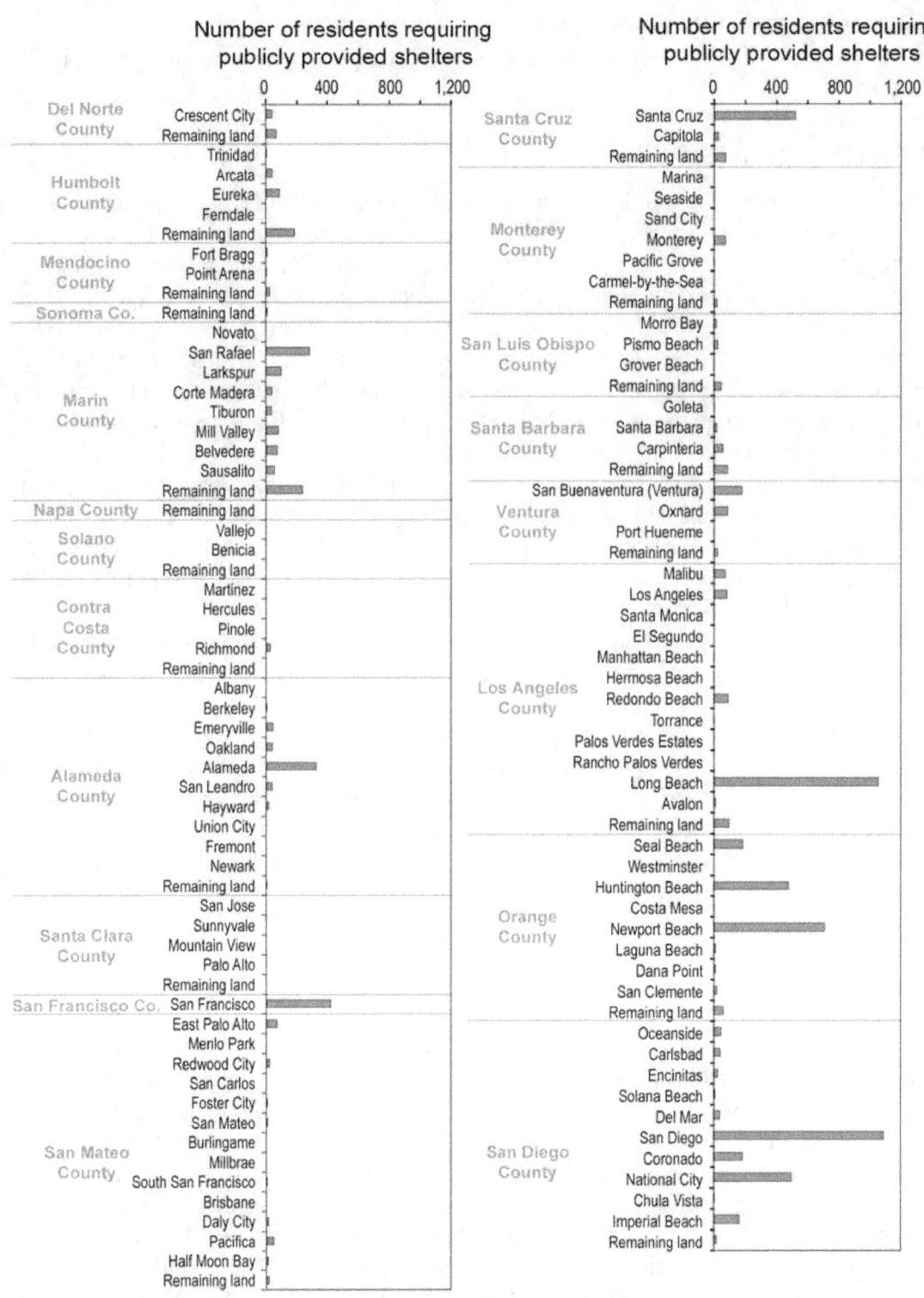

Figure 20. Plot showing number of residents listed by California counties and cities estimated to use public shelters in the SAFRR tsunami scenario. Co., county.

Conclusions

The most significant public-health concern for California coastal communities during a distant-source tsunami is the ability to evacuate people out of the predicted inundation zone. Fatalities from the SAFRR tsunami scenario could be low (and possibly zero) if emergency managers can implement an effective evacuation in the time between tsunami generation and arrival, as well as keep people from entering tsunami-prone areas until all-clear messages can be delivered. This will be challenging given the 91,956 residents, 81,277 employees, as well as numerous public venues, dependent-population facilities, community-support businesses, and high-volume beaches that are in the 79 communities and 17 counties intersected by the scenario tsunami-inundation zone. These evacuation challenges mean that fatalities are possible from the SAFRR tsunami scenario, as well as secondary fatalities, such as vehicular accidents or heart attacks, associated with an evacuation. Although all coastal communities face some level of threat from this scenario, the highest concentrations of people in the tsunami-inundation zone are in Long Beach, San Diego, Newport Beach, Huntington Beach, and San Francisco. Communities also vary in the prevalent categories of populations that are in tsunami-prone areas, such as residents in Long Beach, employees in San Francisco, tourists at public venues in Santa Cruz, and beach or park visitors in unincorporated Los Angeles County.

Certain communities have higher percentages of groups that may need targeted outreach and preparedness training, such as renters, the very young and very old, residents in noninstitutionalized group quarters (for example, military housing and university dormitories), and individuals with limited English-language skills or no English-language skills at all. Sustained education and targeted evacuation messaging is also important at several high-occupancy public venues in the tsunami-inundation zone (for example, city and county beaches, State or national parks, and amusement parks). Education efforts and evacuation coordination for each group should address conditions and needs of the local at-risk population.

Evacuations will be challenging, particularly for certain dependent-care populations, such as patients at hospitals and children at schools and daycare centers. Moving some patients out of a hospital to another facility can take hours to complete, given their existing health conditions. Evacuating schools and childcare centers is easier than evacuating hospitals, but still requires substantial coordination among school officials, parents, and the transportation sector. People living in the tsunami-inundation zone who do not have transportation or who are home-bound need to be identified prior to a tsunami, and plans, including practice drills, should be made for facilitating their evacuation in a timely manner.

In the aftermath of the scenario tsunami, many people may find themselves with damaged homes or businesses. We estimate that approximately 8,678 of the 91,956 residents in the scenario inundation zone are likely to need publicly provided shelters in the short term. In addition, damaged healthcare facilities will impact the public health of the surrounding communities as they seek out other services in the short term. This is also true for any damaged schools or childcare centers, and parents may be unable to return to work until suitable arrangements can be made for their children.

Future Research Needs

Information presented in this report could be used to support emergency, land-use, and resource managers, as well as the coastal communities, in their efforts to identify where additional preparedness and outreach activities may be needed to manage risks associated with California tsunamis. Comparing the number and type of various populations in tsunami-prone areas of California coastal communities is a first step in discussing population vulnerability, but is not an exhaustive statement on the topic because variations in individual sensitivity and adaptive capacity are not fully addressed (Turner and others, 2003). The ability of individuals in a coastal community to prepare for future tsunamis, respond to an event, and recover from an event affects their overall vulnerability to extreme events. Despite similar population distributions, the same extreme natural event would mean a short-term crisis to some and a longer-term disaster to others.

Potential follow-up studies based on results presented here could focus on the adaptive capacity of individuals and communities with regard to their ability to prepare for, respond to, and recover from a damaging tsunami. The current study offers insight into the magnitude of population exposure in the scenario tsunami-inundation zone, and the next steps could focus on the ability of these individuals, as well as the managers and officials responsible for public safety, to manage and reduce their tsunami risks. For example, a gap analysis of local capabilities and capacities could provide emergency managers with a blueprint for where additional training and response planning may be warranted, such as hospitals, schools, childcare centers, and popular tourist destinations. For the healthcare industry, further work may be warranted to determine if vertical evacuation within a building at specific sites is possible, instead of requiring a complete evacuation. With regard to warning-message dissemination, further work may be warranted on determining alternative methods for serving hard-to-reach populations, such as non-English speakers, renters, institutionalized populations, and tourists. Traffic studies for large population centers and for island communities may be warranted to determine whether full evacuations are possible in four hours or less for a distant tsunami. Finally, the substantial difference in the size of at-risk populations in the statewide maximum tsunami-inundation zone and the SAFRR scenario zone suggests a need for a tsunami-scenario catalog to help guide local evacuation decision making efforts.

References Cited

Balaban, V., 2006, Psychological assessment of children in disasters and emergencies: Disasters, v. 30, no. 2, p. 178–198.

Barberopoulou, A., Borrero, J., Uslu, B., Kalligeris, N., Goltz, J., Wilson, R., and Synolakis, C., 2009, New maps of California to improve tsunami preparedness: Eos, American Geophysical Union Transactions, v. 90, no.16, p. 137–144.

Barnard, J., 2011, Dustin Weber, California man, swept to sea by tsunami and presumed dead: Huffington Post, available at http://www.huffingtonpost.com/2011/03/14/dustin-weber-tsunami-dead_n_835236.html.

Barret, A., Hains, A., Jeffries, K., and Yoshida, M., 2012, Monterey Bay Aquarium connections: available at http://www.montereybayaquarium.org/PDF_files/aa/financials/aquarium_annualreview_11.pdf.

Burby, R., Steinberg, L., and Basolo, V., 2003, The tenure trap—The vulnerability of renters to joint natural and technological disasters: Urban Affairs Review, v. 39, no. 1, p. 32–58.

Bureau of Labor Statistics, 2010, United States economy at a glance: U.S. Department of Labor, Bureau of Labor Statistics, available at http://www.bls.gov/oes.

Cal-Atlas Geospatial Clearinghouse, 2013, Cal-Atlas download—Imagery: available at http://www.atlas.ca.gov/download.html#/casil/imageryBaseMapsLandCover/imagery.

California Emergency Management Agency, 2012, Tsunami preparedness: California Emergency Management Agency, available at http://www.calema.ca.gov/PlanningandPreparedness/Pages/Tsunami-Preparedness.aspx.

California Geological Survey, 2012, California geological survey tsunami website: California Geological Survey, available at http://www.conservation.ca.gov/cgs/geologic_hazards/Tsunami/Inundation_Maps/Pages/Index.aspx.

California State Parks, 2010, Statistical report—2009/10 fiscal year: Statewide Planning Unit, Planning Division, California State Parks, available at http://www.parks.ca.gov/pages/795/files/09-10%20statistical%20report%20final%20online.pdf.

Carnival, 2012, Carnival Inspiration cruise ship: available at http://www.carnival.com/cruise-ships/carnival-inspiration.aspx?shipCode=IS.

Catalina Island Chamber of Commerce and Visitors Bureau, 2012, Avalon Bay with cruise ships: Catalina Island Image Library, Catalina Island Chamber of Commerce and Visitors Bureau, website available at http://www.catalinachamber.com/mediafilming/image-library.

City of Huntington Beach, 2012, Residents: California, City of Huntington Beach, available at http://www.huntingtonbeachca.gov/residents/.

Cruisetimetables, 2012, Cruises from Los Angeles 2014: available at http://www.cruisetimetables.com/cruises-from-los-angeles-california-2014.html

Cutter, S., Boruff, B., and Shirley, W., 2003, Social vulnerability to environmental hazards: Social Science Quarterly, v. 84, no. 2, p. 242–261.

Doocy, S., Robinson, C., Moodie, C., and Burnham, G., 2009, Tsunami-related injury in Aceh Province, Indonesia: Global Public Health—An International Journal for Research, Policy and Practice, available at http://www.tandfonline.com/doi/pdf/10.1080/17441690802472612.

Dwight, R., Brinks, M., SharavanaKumar, G., Semenza, J., 2007, Beach attendance and bathing rates for southern California beaches: Ocean and Coastal Management, v. 50, no. 10, p. 847–858.

Enarson, E., and Morrow, B., 1998, The gendered terrain of disaster: Westport, Conn., Praeger, 275 p.

Federal Emergency Management Agency, 2013, Hazus—MH flood technical manual: U.S. Department of Homeland Security, 569 p., available at http://www.fema.gov/library/viewRecord.do?id=4713.

Groves, M., 2008, University of California Los Angeles health center readies move: Los Angeles Times, available at http://articles.latimes.com/2008/jun/25/local/me-ucla25.

Infogroup, 2011, Employer database: Infogroup online dataset, available at http://referenceusagov.com/Static/Home.

Kailes, J., 2009, Emergency power planning for people who use electricity and battery dependent assistive technology and medical devices: available at http://www.jik.com/Power%20Planning%2010.24.09.pdf.

Kuba, M., Dorian, A., Kuljian, S., and Shoaf, K., 2004, Elderly populations in disasters—Recounting evacuation processes from two skilled-care facilities in central Florida: University of Colorado, Boulder, Natural Hazards Center Quick Response Research Report 172, available at http://www.colorado.edu/hazards/research/qr/qr172/qr172.pdf.

Lander, J., Lockridge, P., and Kozuch, M., 1993, Tsunamis affecting the west coast of the United States 1806–1992: National Geophysical Data Center Key to Geophysical Records Documentation No. 29 report, United States Department of Commerce, National Oceanic and Atmospheric Administration, p. 242.

Laska, S., and Morrow, B., 2007, Social vulnerabilities and Hurricane Katrina—An unnatural disaster in New Orleans: Marine Technology Society Journal, v. 40, no. 4, p. 16–26.

Los Angeles Homeless Services Authority, 2011: Greater Los Angeles homeless count report, available at http://www.lahsa.org/docs/2011-Homeless-Count/HC11-Detailed-Geography-Report-FINAL.PDF.

McGuire, L., Ford, E., and Okoro, C., 2007, Natural disasters and older US adults with disabilities—Implications for evacuation: Disasters, v. 31, no. 1, p. 49–56.

Mileti, D., 1999, Disasters by design—A reassessment of natural hazards in the United States: Washington, D.C., Joseph Henry Press, 376 p.

Morrow, B., 1999, Identifying and mapping community vulnerability: Disasters, v. 23, no. 1, p. 1–18.

Nagamatsu, S., Maekawa, T., Ujike, Y., Hashimoto, S., and Fuke, N., 2011, The earthquake and tsunami—Observations by Japanese physicians since the 11 March catastrophe: Critical Care, v. 15, no. 3, 167 p.

National Park Service, 2011, National Park Service Public Use Office: available at http://www.nature.nps.gov/stats/park.cfm.

National Research Council, 2010, Tsunami warning and preparedness—An assessment of the U.S. Tsunami Program and the Nation's preparedness efforts: Committee on the Review of the Tsunami Warning and Forecast System and Overview of the Nation's Tsunami Preparedness, National Academy of Sciences, 266 p.

Ngo, E., 2003, When disasters and age collide—Reviewing vulnerability of the elderly: Natural Hazards Review, v. 2, no. 2, p. 80–89.

Pacific Cruise Ship Terminals, 2012, Cruise links: available at http://www.pcsterminals.com/.

Parson, E., 2002, 1000-year flood paralyzes Texas medical center: Electrical Construction and Maintenance, available at http://ecmweb.com/contractor/1000-year-flood-paralyzes-.

Rother, K., 2001, Surviving the flood—Texas Medical Center's unsinkable spirit: available at http://www.theheart.org/article/178925.do.

Ross, S., Jones, L., Wilson, R., Bahng, B., Barberopoulou, A., Borrero, J., Brosnan, D., Bwarie, J., Geist, E., Johnson, L., Kirby, S., Knight, W., Long, K., Lynett, P., Miller, K., Mortensen, C., Nicolsky, D., Perry, S., Plumlee, G., Porter, K., Real, C., Ryan, K., Suleimani, E., Thio, H., Titov, V., Wein, A., Whitmore, P., Wood, N., The SAFRR (Science Application for Risk Reduction) Tsunami Scenario—Executive Summary and Introduction: U.S. Geological Survey Open-File Report 2013-1170, 29 p.

Schultz, C., Koenig, K., and Lewis, R., 2003, Implications of hospital evacuation after the Northridge, California, Earthquake: New England Journal of Medicine, v. 348, p. 1349–55.

Shoaf, K., and Rottman, S., 2000, Public health impact of disasters: Australian Journal of Emergency Management, v.15, no. 3, p. 58–63.

Titov, V., Gonzales, F., Mofjeld, H., Newman, C., 2001, Project SIFT (Short-term Inundation Forecasting for Tsunamis): International Tsunami Symposium Proceedings, session 7 (7-2), p. 715–721.

Turner, B.L., Kasperson, R.E., Matson, P.A., McCarthy, J.L., Corell, R.W., Christensen, L., Eckley, N., Kasperson, J.X., Luers, A., Martello, M.L., Polsky, C., Pulsipher, A., and Schiller, A., 2003, A framework for vulnerability analysis in sustainability science: Proceedings of the National Academy of Sciences, v. 100, no. 14, p. 8074–8079.

United States Lifesaving Association, 2012, Statistics: United States Lifesaving Association, available at http://arc.usla.org/Statistics/public.asp.

U.S. Census Bureau, 2000, Census tracts and block numbering areas: U.S. Census Bureau, available at http://www.census.gov/geo/www/cen_tract.html.

U.S. Census Bureau, 2010, 2010 TIGER/Line® Shapefiles: U.S. Census Bureau, available at http://www.census.gov/cgi-bin/geo/shapefiles2010/main/.

U.S. Census Bureau, 2012, American FactFinder: U.S. Census Bureau, available at http://factfinder2.census.gov/faces/nav/jsf/pages/index.xhtml.

U.S. Department of Agriculture, 2012, Keeping food safe during an emergency: Food Safety and Inspection Service, available at http://www.fsis.usda.gov/Fact_Sheets/keeping_food_Safe_during_an_emergency/index.asp.

U.S. Geological Survey, 2012, Earthquake "Top 10" Lists & Maps, available at http://earthquake.usgs.gov/earthquakes/eqarchives/.

U.S. Department of Health and Human Services, 2012, At-risk, behavioral health and community resilience (ABC): Office of the Assistant Secretary for Preparedness and Response, available at http://www.phe.gov/Preparedness/planning/abc/Pages/default.aspx.

Visit California, 2012, Media center—The facts: Visit California, available at http://media.visitcalifornia.com/Facts-Learning/The-Facts/.

Westman, A., 2011, Santa Monica Pier visitor counts—Spring and summer 2011: Urban Place Consulting Group, Inc., 10 p.

Wilson, R.I., Admire, A.R., Borrero, J.C., Dengler, L.A., Legg, M.R., Lynett, P., Miller, K.M., Ritchie, A., Sterling, K., McCrink, T.P., and Whitmore, P.M., 2012, Observations and impacts from the 2010 Chilean and 2011 Japanese tsunami in California (USA): Pure and Applied Geophysics, available at http://dx.doi.org/10.1007/s00024-012-0527-z.

Wilson, R.I., Barberopoulou, A., Miller, K.M., Goltz, J.D., and Synolakis, C.E., 2008, New maximum tsunami inundation maps for use by local emergency planners in the State of California, USA [abs.]: Eos, American Geophysical Union Transactions, v. 89, no. 53, Fall Meeting Supplement. Abstract OS43D-1343.

Wilson, R.I., and Miller, K.M., 2012, Improving tsunami hazard mitigation and preparedness using real-time and post-tsunami field data [abs.]: American Geophysical Union Fall Meeting, December 3–7, Abstract NH31C-1614.

Wisner, B., Blaikie, P., Cannon, T., and Davis, I., 2004, At risk—Natural hazards, people's vulnerability and disasters (2nd edition): New York, Routledge, 471 p.

Wood, N., 2007, Variations in city exposure and sensitivity to tsunami hazards in Oregon: U.S. Geological Survey Scientific Investigations Report 2007–5283, 37 p., available at http://pubs.usgs.gov/sir/2007/5283/.

Wood, N., and Good, J., 2004, Vulnerability of a port and harbor community to earthquake and tsunami hazards—The use of GIS in community hazard planning: Coastal Management, v. 32, no. 3, p. 243–269.

Wood, N., Ratliff, J., and Peters, J., 2013, Community exposure to tsunami hazards in California: U.S. Geological Survey Scientific Investigations Report 2012–5222, 49 p.

Appendix A. Estimation of Sheltering Needs

The number of people using publicly provided shelters is estimated in the Hazus-MH MR5 flood loss-estimation methodology (Federal Emergency Management Agency, 2013) by

$$\#STP = \sum_{k=1}^{5} \sum_{m=1}^{3} \ (\alpha_{km} * DP * HI_k * HA_m), \qquad \text{Equation 1}$$

where

$\#STP$ is the number of people using established shelters,
α_{km} is a constant (see below),
DP is displaced population,
HI_k is percentage of population in the kth income class, and
HA_m is percentage of population in mth age class.

Modifying factors based on income and age is represented by the αkm constant and is defined as:

$$\alpha_{km} = (IW \ x \ IM_k) + (AW \ x \ AM_m), \qquad \text{Equation 2}$$

where

IW is Shelter Category Weight for Income (default value is 0.80),
AW is Shelter Category Weight for Age (default value is 0.20),
IM_k is Relative Modification Factor for Income (values in table A1), and
AM_m is Relative Modification Factor for Age (values in table A1).

Table 1. Relative modification factors used to estimate sheltering needs

Category	Class	Description	Default for Communities with 60% or More of Households with Income >$35,000
Income	IM_1	Household income < $10,000	0.46
Income	IM_2	$10,000 < Household income < $15,000	0.36
Income	IM_3	$15,000 < Household income < $25,000	0.12
Income	IM_4	$25,000 < Household income < $35,000	0.05
Income	IM_5	$35,000 < Household income	0.01
Age	AM_1	Population less than 16 years old	0.05
Age	AM_2	Population between 16 and 65 years old	0.2
Age	AM_3	Population more than 65 years old	0.5